PREACHING WITHOUT NOTES

A SERIES OF LECTURES

BY

RICHARD S. STORRS, D.D., LL.D.

HODDER & STOUGHTON
NEW YORK
GEORGE H. DORAN COMPANY

CONTENTS.

	PAGE
First Lecture	9
Second Lecture	70
Third Lecture	131
Appendix	209

PREFATORY NOTE.

In marking out the course of thought to be pursued in the following lectures the writer of this note had no more intention of preparing a volume, however slight, on the best method of preaching the Gospel, than he had of composing a treatise on Ethics, or an essay on Fine Art. His only design was, in compliance with the invitation of the honored President and Faculty of the Union Theological Seminary, to say some words to the students of that institution, especially to those of the senior class, on his own experience in preaching without notes, and on the lessons which this had taught him as to the most effective mode of preparing for the work.

The one lecture which at first was contemplated grew into three; and if the three had been multiplied by three, the subject would have remained inadequately treated. It was not till after the first of them had been delivered that the lecturer was advised, by the present publisher, that arrangements had been made for fully reporting them, and that, unless positive objection were made, they would be printed. Certainly no book was ever made, therefore, with less of pre-determination on the part of the author.

It seems only reasonable to ask that any one into whose hands the book may fall will remember the way in which it came to exist, and will not expect from it something more and other than it seeks to supply. The lectures were spoken, without having been written; and the author would not have felt at liberty to recast them, even if he had had the leisure for the work. Here and there a phrase or a sentence has been changed; a word has occasionally been substituted for another, when that selected at the instant of speaking seemed not the best as more quietly reviewed; and in one instance an unimportant paragraph has been transferred from one part of a lecture to another more fitting. Otherwise, the lectures are printed as delivered,—this being the wish of all concerned with them.

The style of them is, therefore, so entirely without the elaboration in which authors delight that if pride of authorship alone were to be consulted they certainly would not now be published. But the thoughts expressed in them are such as had commended themselves to the lecturer, in his own ministerial life and work, and such as he therefore had no hesitation in presenting to others, in the form of free and familiar discourse. He does not now shrink from presenting them to the public, though quite aware how slight is their claim to any general attention, and how different would have been the form to be given them if he had contemplated making a book.

They are published, at the expressed desire of some who had heard them, and of more who had not; in the hope that, with all their obvious imperfections, they may contribute something, of encouragement if not of more special assistance, to those who would speak the unchanging truth with which God crowds and crowns the Gospel, out of a furnished and quickening mind, without that perpetual bondage to the pen which presses heavily on many ministers.

RICHARD S. STORRS.

BROOKLYN, February 15, 1875.

FIRST LECTURE.

Mr. President: Young Gentlemen:—

There will be no misunderstanding between us, I presume, as to my general purpose and plan in coming hither, or in what I am to say to you, now and hereafter. I do not come, of course, to deliver systematic and elaborate lectures, on the subject upon which I am to speak. You have Professors to do that; with leisure, skill, and an aptness for the office, which I do not possess; and I should only be intruding myself upon their function, without invitation and without warrant, if I were to attempt any thing of the kind. I have come simply to talk to you a little, in a familiar way, of the conditions of success in preaching without notes; and to offer some thoughts, concerning these conditions, which are suggested to me by my own experience.

I have thought, in looking back on my Seminary course, that I should have been glad if some one who had entered the ministry before me had then told me, frankly and fully, as I hope to tell you, what he had learned by any efforts which he had made in this direction. So I have cheerfully accepted the invitation to do for you what I see I should have been glad to have had some one else then do for me.

I am somewhat abashed, I confess, at finding so many present whom I have not come prepared to address: Professors, Secretaries, Clergymen, Lawyers, Editors, and others — many of them masters of every art and power of eloquence, as I am not, and far better qualified to instruct me on the subject than I am to give suggestions to them. But I shall not be diverted from the one purpose which has brought me hither — to talk familiarly and freely to you. If what I am to say shall seem common-place, as very likely it will, to these gentlemen whose presence I did not anticipate, I can only remind them that they are not here at my invitation, and that if they choose to take part of their purgatory in this life, and in this particular fashion, we cannot object. But I have only you to speak to; and shall not turn aside to consider whether that which is in my mind is, or is not, what they have come to hear.

As I said, the suggestions which I make will be largely those derived from my personal experience. I do not know that you will find much profit in them, for I remember the remark of Coleridge that 'experience is like the stern-light of a ship at sea: it enlightens only the track which has been passed over.' There are such differences between men, in temperament, habit, mental constitution, the natural and customary methods of work, that the experience of one may not suggest much of value to another, and I shall not be disappointed if mine is not very serviceable to you. Indeed this matter of speaking freely to a public assembly, without notes, is eminently one in regard to which every man must learn for himself; and no one can make his own method a rule for another, unless he can simultaneously exchange minds with him — a thing which in our case would be neither possible for me, nor perhaps profitable for you. Still: the rules which experience suggests are likely to be better than those which theorists elaborate in their libraries; and I have got more help myself from hints of others, working in the same direction, than from any discussions in learned treatises. So I shall give you what I can, and hope for the best; and if any thing which I may say shall prove to be of service to you, I shall be amply rewarded for the work.

To lay the foundation for my remarks I will state rapidly what my experience in the matter has been.

I was in part educated for the bar; and was at one time quite familiar with the Boston court-rooms, at a period when the Suffolk-bar was at the height of its power and fame. Mr. Webster was there, in the intervals between the sessions of the Senate, in the maturity and splendor of his majestic intelligence. Mr. Choate was there — under whose direction I was prosecuting my studies — whose genius seemed an oriental exotic, brilliant, luxuriant, among the common ferns and brake of New England. Mr. Benjamin R. Curtis was there, — recently deceased, then in the prime of his force and his career, — whose power of perspicuous and persuasive legal statement surpassed that, I think, of any speaker whom I have since anywhere heard. With these were associated others, not so prominent then or since before the public, but only second to them in faculty and in training.

All these men, of course, were in the habit of speaking constantly, without notes, before the full Bench, or to the Jury; in the most important and difficult cases, as well as in those of lighter consequence; when arguing difficult questions of law, as well as when discussing an issue of facts. I never knew but one lawyer who was in the habit of reading his arguments from a full manuscript; and he, though an able, was a remarkably timid man, whose argument was always addressed to the Judge, not to the Jury.

I could not see, therefore, why a minister — however limited in faculty and in culture, in comparison certainly with these eminent men — should not do that before his congregation, which lawyers were doing all the time in the courts; and when my plans of life were changed, under the impulse as I thought of God's Spirit, and I had devoted myself to the ministry, I determined if possible to fit myself to do this, and to preach without reading. It seemed to me that this was the more apostolic way, at least. I could not learn that Paul pulled out a Greek manuscript, and undertook to read it with his infirm eyes, when he addressed the woman at Philippi; or even when he spoke on Mars Hill, under the shadow of the Propylea and the Parthenon, to the critical Athenians. It seemed to me that to speak to men without notes, out of a full and earnest mind, was now as then the most natural and effective way to address them; the way most fitting to those sublime and practical themes which the preacher of the Gospel has to present, and to the interests, so immensely important, which he is to subserve. And I was distinctly and deliberately determined, if it was in my power to accomplish it, to learn to speak thus, and not to either read my sermons, or write them out and commit them to memory.

Accordingly, I did some training for this in my Seminary course; but it was not much, nor was it particularly fruitful of good. I presume that you are here encouraged in such efforts, guided, and stimulated. I presume the students at Andover are so now, under the present *régime*. But in my time there — as some of these gentlemen present will remember, who were there with me — such a method of preaching was not looked upon with particular favor. The atmosphere of the Seminary was not friendly or helpful to it. It was about as trying an ordeal as a man can well pass to stand up and speak without a manuscript, in the lecture-room or the chapel. I don't know that the criticism which was encountered was any more severe than it should have been. I am sure it was never intentionally oppressive or unjust. But it was most thoroughly searching and exact; so that if a man had any weaknesses or faults about him, as all of us had, he was sure enough to find them out, and was usually glad, after one experiment, to take refuge in future behind his notes.

I got some practice in the debating society; and two or three times, as I remember, adventured upon short public speeches, without notes in my pocket. But on the whole I lost rather than gained, in this regard, in my Seminary course; and when I came out was hardly as eager, perhaps, so far as courage and confidence were concerned, was hardly as well fitted, to preach without notes as I should have been earlier. My conviction on the subject remained, however; and I was still resolved to get used to this method, and to employ it, if I could.

My first settlement in the ministry was at Brookline, near Boston; in a charming suburban parish, but with a congregation not helpful to my plans in regard to this matter of the method of preaching. In a church capable of holding five hundred or six hundred people we had usually, in the winter, a congregation of perhaps seventy-five to a hundred. They were as affectionate and appreciative hearers as any man need ask or hope for. But the majority of them were cultured, careful, critical hearers, who required a high intellectual tone in whatever was said to them, and were instantly sensitive to its absence.

They had been trained under the Boston pulpits, the ministers in which almost universally — perhaps quite universally — then read their sermons; and, though kind as they could be, they were inevitably exacting in their demand for precision and elegance of literary form. It was a scattered assembly, of individuals, and of separated households. There was no mass of hearers, to be kindled and swayed by a common enthusiasm, and in turn to reäct upon the preacher: they were not numerous enough for that, and the building itself was relatively too large. They were most of them, of course, older than I was, and I was diffident in speaking before them on subjects much longer familiar to them than they had been to me. They were more or less anxious, too, as to the impression to be made by my preaching on the Unitarian or Episcopalian outsiders who frequently made a part of the congregation; and so were uneasy and apprehensive when I rose without notes, and jubilant whenever they saw these before me.

I made my endeavors, more than once, to carry out the plan which I had proposed, and preach without a manuscript before me; but it was all the time like swimming up the rapids, while with the manuscript I had only to float easily on the current. I tried to combine the advantages of both methods: to have notes before me, a somewhat full skeleton of my discourse, and then to be at liberty, in the intervals between the heads and sub-heads, to avail myself of any suggestions that might come. But this plan I found, for me — however it may be for others — the poorest possible. I lost all fluency, and continuity of thought. The intervals were not long enough, between my prepared heads, to allow the mind to get freely, freshly, vigorously at work. Just as my mental glow began, if it did begin, it had to be checked by returning to the manuscript. My utterance was inevitably interrupted, suspended, at the moment at which it might otherwise have come to be easy and spontaneous. I could never get force enough, between the recurring references to my notes, to push the sermon home upon my hearers, or even to carry my own mind through it with any sense of liberty and vigor. The whole sermon became a series of jerks. There was no gathered and helpful momentum, toward the end, or anywhere else. I lost the foresight of the end from the beginning; was wholly engrossed in taking each successive step correctly, when I should come to it. I became timid, retrospective, and had no sense of real mastery over the theme, or of any mastery whatever over the minds to which I was speaking.

So I gave up that plan, then and there, and have never once thought of trying it since. It would be to me like running a race, with a ball and chain attached to each foot. I should read every sermon I ever preached, if that were to be the only alternative.

During the year which I spent at Brookline, I persevered in these efforts to get free from necessary dependence on my notes; but I do not think that I ever once, in the pulpit there, on the Sunday, had any true sense of liberty and joy in public utterance, unless I was reading. It was a steady hard struggle, from first to last, for conscious freedom in public speech; with almost no sense of success, and with very little reward, except as my will got hardened by it. I don't know whether I should have kept on or not, if I had stayed there longer.

It so happened that the first sermon which I ever preached at Brooklyn — the only one, indeed, which I ever preached there before being called to the Church of the Pilgrims — was preached without notes. I was called upon unexpectedly for the service, as I was passing through the city, and when I had with me no manuscript sermons. But I had a subject in mind on which I had written not long before, in which I had been at the time much interested, and of which I had made a thorough analysis. The course of thought pursued in the sermon was fresh in my mind, though the notes were not with me. I preached in a lecture-room, which was wholly filled with attentive hearers. I had no sort of fear of the congregation, which was entirely made up of strangers to me; and I found as I went on, in the treatment of the subject with which I had made myself previously familiar, that the mind worked with a facility, a force, a sense of exhilaration, which I never had had in reading from a manuscript. I enjoyed the service, and had a certain sense of Christian success in it. The people were interested; and their interest had an instant reflex influence upon my own mind, so that the success became duplicated. It seemed to me, at the end, that it must be always easy and pleasant, under similar conditions, to repeat that experiment.

When, therefore, I was called to that church, and had decided to go there, I was fully determined to carry out this plan of preaching without notes, occasionally at least, at all hazards. I was twenty-five years old, and thought I knew something: — as men are apt to think, at that time of life. I had had a year's practice in the pulpit, such as it was, and had gained some freedom and confidence from it. The congregation at Brooklyn was certainly larger than the one to which I had ministered before, and it seemed to me likely to be more sympathetic with a freer tone and style of speech. I was more certain than ever that I should find relief and help in my preferred method of preaching, if I could master it; and I was resolved to master it, if the thing could be done.

So the first sermon which I preached, after my Installation, was preached without notes. It was very nearly a dead failure. It *was* an absolute failure, so far as any sense of liberty on my part, or any useful effect on the people, was concerned. I have the notes of it still; and not long ago, in looking over old papers, I happened upon these, and read them over. I saw at a glance what the secret of the failure had been. I had made too much preparation in detail; had written out heads, sub-divisions, even some passages or paragraphs in full, in order that I might be certain beforehand to have material enough at command; and the result of it was that I was all the time looking backward, not forward, in preaching; trying to remember, not only prearranged trains of thought but particular forms of expression, instead of trusting to the impulse of the subject, and seeking to impress certain great and principal features of it on the congregation.

My verbal memory has always been the weakest part of my mental organization. I hardly dare trust myself now to quote a sentence from any writer, without having it before me in manuscript. I had wholly overloaded this verbal memory, in my preparation for the service; and the inevitable consequence was that it and I staggered along together, for perhaps twenty-five minutes, and then stopped. I sank back on the chair, almost wishing that I had been with Pharaoh and his hosts when the Red Sea went over them! The people were disappointed, and I was nearly sick. I am quite certain that if the proposal to invite me to Brooklyn had been made subsequently to that, instead of before it, I never should have been called to *that* congregation! I went back to the reading of manuscript sermons, and doubted for a good while if I should ever again try another method. I could not hazard another mortification so keen as that, or another failure so complete.

However, after a time, the old feeling revived, and it seemed a shame to give it up so. I always preached my weekly lectures without notes, or with only brief ones ; and that helped and encouraged me to again try it in the church, as swimming in the pond helps one by-and-by to swim out fearlessly in the open sea. I was in the habit, too, of making occasional addresses, as other clergymen did, on public anniversary occasions ; and in giving these, as we always did, without notes, it was continually anew impressed upon me that it must be possible to do the same in the pulpit, and that there would come with it a certain increase of independence and of power.

I remember an occasion, for example — it must have been twenty-four or five years ago —

in the old Broadway Tabernacle, at an anniversary of the Bible Society, when I had a conscious pleasure and freedom in speaking, an invigoration of mind in the very process of speaking, which reading from a manuscript never had given. The subject was one familiar to me, through my connection at that time with the Committee of Versions. The occasion was an important one: the assembly was very large, crowding the platform, filling the house, absolutely. It was a responsive, sympathetic assembly, full of a diffused enthusiasm which attracted and rewarded whatever was said that was worth being heard. There was a pull from without, as well as an incessant push from within. The audience and the speaker reäcted on each other. A man could hardly help speaking easily, joyfully, in such surroundings; and I wished afterward, oftentimes, that the same experience which one now and then thus gained upon the platform could be transferred to the pulpit, and could there become customary.

After a time there came a growing religious interest, working and widening throughout the congregation; and that helped greatly to preach without a manuscript. The people were more moved by the more direct address, and welcomed it eagerly. My own mind was more quick with a vivid realization of the meaning and the importance of the Divine message. It acted more ardently and intensely upon subjects, and found it more natural to speak of these in words which had not been preärranged by the pen. Preacher and people were all lifted by the impulse, as the steamship is carried over the bar by the swelling tide which imperceptibly swings it upward. They were more sympathetic; I was more strongly moved by my subjects, and more intent on practical results: and so I began to get hold of them, at last, in this mode of preaching. Individuals would now and then tell me of impressions made on them, or on their friends, of helps given, of new thoughts started, of words that had become warnings or motives; and more frequently than not these had come from sermons unwritten. So, though far from feeling at ease, as an habitual thing, when I entered the pulpit without my notes, I had an occasional sense of success in dispensing with them, and began to do it with more and more of facility and of confidence.

When I speak of "success," Gentlemen, you will of course understand me as speaking only of relative success; of success, as compared with previous failure. Nobody can be more perfectly aware than I am that in no other than this limited and personal sense have I ever reached "success;" and there seems a certain unwarrantable assumption in my speaking to you of its conditions. But the navigator may know the route which must be taken to reach the North Pole, though he himself has never been there; and so I think that I have learned what are the necessary conditions of a success which is far enough from my attainment.

I used now and then, at the time I refer to, to

have this occasional, partial sense, of a relative success, in preaching without notes.

But I was still always embarrassed by a degree of uncertainty as to how far I should be able in the pulpit to develop my subject; and the amount of the previous preparation which I had made appeared to give no measure and no prophecy of the freedom in preaching which I should enjoy. In fact, the two seemed often to stand in an inverse ratio; so that the more ample the preparation, the more meagre and unsatisfactory might be the discourse. I almost always approached the service, therefore, with a distinct timidity; and was careful to preach without notes in the morning, if at all, when I had most of freshness and strength, and when I knew of the written sermon held in reserve, on which I could fall back for the second service, — thus redeeming in part any special failure which the morning might witness.

This went on for a number of years; till at last, a dozen years ago or so, after I had been in

Brooklyn for sixteen or seventeen years, I began to feel that growing sense of the oppressiveness of routine, and that teasing desire for a change of field, which almost every minister feels after many years of continuous service in the same parish. It seemed to me that the people were getting so accustomed to my ways of conceiving and presenting truth that they were now insensitive to them; and that some decided change in the teaching mind would be to them of service. But that was not the worst of it. I felt myself getting into ruts, in regard to my method of treating subjects, my modes of argument, expression, illustration. It seemed to me that the mind itself was in danger of drying up; that it needed a decided and positive change, to give it impulse, vivacity, flexibility, and to prevent it from becoming rigid and narrow. In other words, I was growing restless; and was nearly persuaded that the people would be better for a new mind in the pulpit, and that I should be better for another field of labor. If it had been easy and right for me to leave my parish, and take another, I should almost certainly then have done so. But in the existing circumstances of my church I did not feel at liberty to leave it; and the case was one of those in regard to which one has to consider, you know, what Professor Stuart used to call the *terminus ad quem* as well as the *terminus a quo.* So, as I had neither liberty to leave, nor any special invitation to go elsewhere, it seemed plainly my duty to stay where I was, and to find some other way of overcoming the tendencies which had begun to embarrass me.

The only way that I could think of was to make a decided change in my method of working; to do thenceforth habitually, what until then I had done only occasionally; and to make it thereafter my principal aim, in my public ministry, to present subjects to the congregation without immediate help from a manuscript. This involved important changes in my whole way of working, both before preaching, and in it;

and I thought might have the effect which I desired, on the people, and on myself.

I communicated my purpose, privately, to a number of the principal members of the congregation, and gave them my reasons for it. They were abundantly satisfied with the decision. It came to be generally understood, before long, that a written sermon was never to be expected in the morning; and after that I was not embarrassed by any surprise on the part of my hearers when they saw me open the Bible, and begin the discourse, without paper before me. I still wrote for the evening-service; but that gradually became less important in comparison with the morning, and the far larger part of my time and force was given to the sermon which was to be preached without a manuscript.

From that time I had more and more of facility and freedom in preaching in this way. The people became accustomed to it, and most of them preferred it. Those who came later into the congregation, found me established in the practice, and expected nothing else. And so that method was finally fixed, for one service on every Sunday.

After a number of years of this practice, in 1869, while our church-edifice was being reconstructed, my congregation was thrown for many months into the Academy of Music for its place of worship. The seats there were all free; and the assemblies, gathered from all parts of the town, especially in the evening, were large and very miscellaneous. One of the Professors in the Divinity School at Cambridge, who was remonstrated with for leaving his chair of theological instruction in order to take a seat in Congress, is said to have replied, that perhaps the objector was not quite aware what the extent of his opportunity was as a teacher of theology. 'There were indeed three men in his class: one of them was a sceptic, one a dyspeptic, and the third a Swedenborgian.' Well, I had all these, and a great many of other sorts and conditions, from the most devout and intelligent of worshippers to the most entirely indifferent and careless, with a larger proportion of unbelievers than is commonly to be found in a Sunday congregation.

It was simply idle to try to hold the attention of an audience so various, promiscuous, and untrained as that, while reading from a manuscript. Numbers of them would have laughed in my face, and have left the house. Certainly, they would never have come a second time. Inserting a manuscript between them and myself, would have been like cutting the telegraph-wires, and putting a sheet of paper into the gap. See if you then can send your message on the wire! The electricity would not pass. So I gave up the manuscript on the spot, the first night, and preached thenceforth both morning and evening without any notes. I have never written but one sermon since; and that was for a special occasion, outside altogether of my own congregation.

It is an entire mistake to suppose, as some

have done, that I broke down in health in consequence of this change, or in consequence of the new work in the Academy, and of the strain which came with it. That was due wholly to other causes, and many things contributed to it. I had been preaching for twenty-five years, with only the brief summer-vacations in all that time. I had had a large, an always increasing, pastoral work. For thirteen years I had been one of the editors of a leading religious newspaper. I had for many of those years been in the habit of lecturing often, during the winter. I had freely accepted public responsibilities, some of which brought much labor with them, in the city which I live in. I was nearly at the end of all my resources, of strength and nerve-force, when we began reconstructing the church; and that brought with it its own anxieties and burdensome cares. During the winter at the Academy I had a succession of prostrating colds, which left me at last at a very low point of vital energy. In the summer which followed, after we had returned to the church, I was visited with sudden and heavy domestic grief, from whose shock and shadow I could not rally. I was simply worn out, with severe, long-protracted, unremitting hard work; and I then did, what I should have done years before, except for my father's advanced age, and my desire to be near him — I went to Europe, for a year and more, to let the exhausted forces rally, and give nature a chance to restore the excessive vital waste.

I returned from Europe refreshed, as I had hoped, in body and in mind, and resumed my work according to the method which I have described; and have maintained it, as I said, ever since. Instead of breaking me down, it had enabled me, I am certain, to go on at least a year or two longer than I otherwise could have done; and neither the people nor I had the least desire for any change in it. I shall certainly never depart from it hereafter, while I continue to preach at all.

I am afraid, Gentlemen, that you will think I

have dwelt too long on this common-place experience of mine; but I have been asked to give you such suggestions as grow out of this, and so it seemed needful to tell you at the outset just what it had been. It is very unimportant, except as it gives me a certain right, perhaps, to speak of the relative advantages of the two modes of preaching — with notes, and without them. I hope I have not seemed egotistical in it, for my only desire is to serve and help you; and for that purpose, only, I have delayed upon the matter. I wrote for many years, fully, and carefully. I now write only a brief outline of the discourse, covering usually one or two sheets of common note-paper, and have no notes before me in the pulpit — not a line, or a catch-word. So I think I know how the one method operates, and how the other, on both preacher and people; and I see — certainly more clearly than I used to — what is necessary to one's success if he would address a public assembly without committing to memory what he says, and without aid from present notes. The ideal of that success we may none of us realize. But I think we may all of us make some approach to it, if we earnestly try.

Now for some general suggestions, growing out of this experience, which I shall present as preliminary to others, more detailed and specific, that I design to offer hereafter.

FIRST, let me say: *Never begin to preach without notes with any idea of saving yourselves work by it.* — If you do, you will fail; and you will richly deserve to fail. Any suspicion of this among your people will destroy your hold on them. Your own minds will deteriorate; and your sermons will lose, not finish only, but body and vigor.

Of course there is a certain amount of nervous fatigue connected with the compulsory use of the pen — especially of a steel-pen, a gold-pen, or any other with an inflexible handle — which is saved when a man only writes as he feels like it, and not under pressure: and this is an important gain to one who has been emancipated from notes. There is a gain in release from confining desk-work, and from constant bondage to prescribed hours. A man who writes his sermons fully sometimes becomes so wearied with the intent application of eye and hand, while making the manuscript, that he hardly can rally to deliver the sermon with as much of glow as he gave it in writing. One who trains his mind to work without the pen finds, after a while, that he can meditate his discourses while he is walking; while he is doing errands; while he is sitting in the parlor, waiting for the friend on whom he is calling. The whole plan of a sermon will sometimes shape itself suddenly in his mind. Thoughts come to him more and more freely, at odd moments; and sometimes these are the best he gets, as Goethe said that his best thoughts came: 'like singing birds, the free children of God, crying 'here we are!'' Of course this is not confined to one who preaches without notes. It is true also of one who is closely engaged in preparing a manuscript. But I think this habit of mind is more common where one meditates subjects without dependence on pencil or pen. Certainly I know that such thoughts now come to me oftener than they did when I always had a manuscript lying in the study, impatient to be finished.*

But, on the other hand, whatever of time and of force is saved, in these ways or in others, must only be more carefully devoted to the complete conscious mastery of the subject which one intends to present, if he is to speak without notes; so that he knows it thoroughly, has searched it through, is vitally charged with it, and has it fully and vividly in mind. This is absolutely indispensable to any real success in presenting it to others; and this implies a concentrated, continuous, intense action of your mind upon it,— more so, I think, than you would ordinarily give if writing upon it. One does not usually, I suspect, get his whole plan, in all its bearings, fully in

* Note I.

mind, before the process of writing begins. But he must do this before he speaks, if he is to speak with any proper success.

Then, for a long time, one must expect a degree of mental excitement, and of consequent mental exhaustion, in uttering his sermon, when preaching without notes, which does not attend the reading of a manuscript. At the outset, at any rate, the reader has much the easier task in the matter of delivery. Having read his sermon, of thirty-five or forty minutes, he is generally fresh enough to read it again, if there were occasion. It is far more exhausting to speak the same thoughts, with no notes before you. Much more of vital force goes out, in the rapid and continuing action of all your powers on what you are saying. But, remember, that here is a recompense as well as a demand. For this essential vital force, going forth on one's speech, is that which makes words life and spirit. It is, under God, the converting force, which quickens, sways, inspires those to whom it is sent, as thought alone can never do

It is the power which God employs as His great moral instrument in the world.

Such abundant and careful preliminary preparation, and such a vital absorption of the mind in the subject while preaching, are needed to conciliate the attention, the respect, the confidence of your hearers. They will be repulsed, and with reason, you will lose all your hold on them — they will swiftly antagonize you, with indifference or hostility — if they come to suspect that you are simply shirking labor in preaching without writing. This is in fact one chief reason, their suspicion of this, why people are often uneasy and restless under such preaching. My father was a clergyman of the old school, accustomed always to write for the pulpit with studious care. He was ready, free, eloquent in speech, in the lecture-room, or on the platform. Some of the most stirring and animating addresses that I ever heard from human lips I have heard from him, in small assemblies, on special occasions. But I think that to the end of his life he always wrote every word of all his sermons; and, for a long time, he looked with great distrust on my preferred method of preaching. One of his remarks was, frequently repeated: "My son, I was early taught that I must bring beaten oil into the sanctuary;" and I never could persuade him that there was any better way of beating it than by using a pen for a spoon! So, for years, after I was much in the habit of preaching without notes at home, I always carried written sermons to Braintree, and read them, as well as I could, in his pulpit.

It happened, however, on a special occasion, that he was very desirous that I should preach when I had no manuscript with me. I was obliged to take, therefore, the same method to which I had been accustomed at home; and having, as far as I could, charged my mind with the subject, I spoke without notes. After that, he would never let me do any thing else, when I preached for him. He saw that the subject had been carefully considered; that the sermon was not being hastily manufactured, on the spot, but was the result of serious preceding reflection and study: and that was all that he needed to know. Then, he yielded to the influence of the freer and more forceful spontaneous utterance, and even regretted that he had not himself adopted the same method, earlier in life. So, you see, Gentlemen, I have made at least one convert!

Such persistent and strenuous mental exertion on your subjects is needful, too, to your own mind, to discipline, widen, invigorate that, and make it fit to master themes, and speak to men. Whoever has thoroughly mastered one subject, will thereby be fitted to grapple others: but a kind of general mental flabbiness is the sure result of any let-up from austere and exacting mental discipline. Never suffer yourselves, therefore, to speak, as Strafford said, 'from the teeth, outward.' Your speech will certainly become stale, flat, and unprofitable, if you do. Conceive your subject clearly, get hold of it firmly, let your mind be thoroughly charged and vitalized with the proper force of it; let the sentiment which it inspires, and the action which it prompts, allure, incite, possess your souls; and then speak, out of the fulness of your mind, with a heart warmed by the truth you have considered, and which you now are eager to present.

And, SECONDLY: *Always be careful to keep up the habit of writing, with whatever of skill, elegance, and force, you can command.*

You will need this for the enlarging and refining of your vocabulary, if for nothing else. Without it, you will almost certainly fall into the habit of using cheap and common words; and of using even these with only a rough approximation to their meaning, with no subtle or precise discrimination between them. Mr. Choate once said to one of his students: "You don't want a diction gathered from the newspapers, caught from the air, common and unsuggestive;

but you want one whose every word is full-freighted with suggestion and association, with beauty and power." * Some words contain a whole history in themselves. Panic, — it carries us back to the day of Marathon. Panegyric, Pasquinade — there are multitudes of such words, opulent, microcosmic, in which histories are imaged, which record civilizations. Others recall to us great passages of eloquence, or of noble poetry, and bring in their train the whole splendor of such passages, when they are uttered.†

We cannot be always using such words. The plainer are better, for common service. But when these richer, remoter words, come into the discourse, they make it ample and royal. They are like glistening threads of gold, interwoven with the commoner tissue. There is a certain spell in them, for the memory, the imagination. Elect hearers will be warmed and won by them. But we cannot get such words, and keep them,

* Parker's Reminiscences: p. 249.

† Note II.

except by writing. Reading will put them into our hands. Only careful writing separates, signalizes, infixes them in the mind, makes them our possession forever. We pass over them, as we read. We pick them out, with the pen.*

So always be careful to write, habitually: not sermons, necessarily; essays, analyses, articles for papers, lectures if you like — whatever most attracts you to the use of the pen.

You will need the constant discipline of such writing to enable you to form sentences rapidly and securely, — sentences which shall be firm, well-proportioned, consistent, complete. Nothing is more absolutely fatal to the impression of a spoken discourse than a succession of halting broken-backed sentences. They are like broken-winged birds, hindering the flight of the whole flock; almost like broken rails on the track, which fling the entire train into a heap. When subject and predicate, protasis and apodosis, are jumbled together in inextricable confusion, or

* Notes III. and IV.

are hopelessly disjointed from each other, no one will long try to follow the speaker. At the beginning of every sentence one should be able to look to the end of it, that he himself may be carried on, and his hearers with him, with ease and steadiness, to its foreseen conclusion.

Not all men have the wit and wisdom of Father Taylor, the famous preacher to sailors in Boston. It is told of him that once getting involved in a sentence, where clause after clause had been added to each other, and one had branched off in this direction and another in that, till he was hopelessly entangled, and the starting point was quite out of sight, he paused, and shook himself free of the perplexity by saying: "Brethren, I don't know exactly where I went in, in beginning this sentence; and I don't in the least know where I'm coming out; but one thing I *do* know, I'M BOUND FOR THE KINGDOM OF HEAVEN!" So he took a wholly new departure, and left the broken-backed centipede of a sentence lying where it might, in the track behind him. Perhaps that is as good a way as any of getting out of such confusion, if one ever is caught in it. But it is better never to be so caught. Father Taylor himself could not have repeated the experiment often.

Sentences may be either long or short, simple or complex, but they should always be essentially periodic, having a beginning, a middle, and an end; and the habit of forming them easily, naturally, comes with the diligent use of the pen.*

One needs too this discipline of careful writing to systematize his thoughts; to make his analysis of subjects, or his arrangement of arguments, clear, enlightening, satisfactory.

Without this, he will be constantly in danger of falling into the habit of loose, vague, ineffectual thinking, — if it can be called thinking, at all — with no sharpness, or system, or synthesis in it. The pen gives march to the mind. It teaches exactness, discrimination, and helps the whole constructive faculty. It is a great

* Note V.

educator. Better give up half your library than let the pen fall into disuse. In fact your library will lose more than half its value, unless you use the pen to represent and preserve the results of your reading. You must not, fumble over subjects, but grasp them; not glance at them, but resolve them: and the pen is the instrument with which to do it.

Dr. Channing has some admirable words on the benefits of composition to the writer himself, which I will read if you allow me — though I know how hazardous it is to introduce his polished periods into the midst of a talk like this. He says: "We doubt whether a man ever brings his faculties to bear with their whole force on a subject, until he writes upon it. . . . By attempting to seize his thoughts, and fix them in an enduring form, he finds them vague and unsatisfactory, to a degree which he did not suspect, and toils for a precision and harmony of views, of which he never before felt the need. He places his subject in new lights; submits it to a searching analysis; compares and connects it with his various knowledge; seeks for it new illustrations and analogies; weighs objections; and, through these processes, often arrives at higher truths than he at first aimed to illustrate. Dim conceptions grow bright. Glorious thoughts, which had darted as meteors through the mind, are arrested, and gradually shine with a sun-like splendor, with prolific energy, on the intellect and heart. . . . Even when composition yields no such fruits, it is still a great intellectual help. It always favors comprehensive and systematical views. The laborious distribution of a great subject, so as to assign to each part or topic its just position and due proportion, is singularly fitted to give compass and persevering force of thought." *

There is profound truth in these words. They ought to be always borne in mind by one who is training himself to speak without notes He must discipline his mind by the use of the pen,

* Channing's W)rks, vol. i. pp. 263, 264.

that the thoughts which subsequently rise to his lips may be sound and clear, and worth the uttering. Nothing but the pen can break up books for us, and transmute them into personal knowledge and thought.*

And further, THIRDLY: *Be perfectly frank with your people in regard to this matter of your method of preaching;* so putting yourselves at once in right relations with them about it.

Let them know that you design to preach without notes, and without memorizing the sermon; and give them your reasons. Tell them that you have the strongest conviction that your business in the pulpit is not to read essays, but to fill your mind with clear, profound, quickening impressions of those sublime truths which the Gospel reveals, and then to declare these to the congregation, as the Spirit of God shall give you utterance. Ask them to bear with you, if at first you seem to fail to do justice to your subject, or to your own thought of it; and

* Note VI.

to wait with patience until you are stronger, and are able more fully to instruct and inspire them, for the worship of God. So you will have a free field for your effort, and be unembarrassed by their reluctance or their surprise.

Many eminent clergymen speak admirably in the lecture-room, or on the platform, who are abashed and disconcerted in the pulpit, if they have not a manuscript, because of their consciousness that there the people expect this.

The best debater whom I ever heard among American ministers — if I should mention his name all who know him would assent to the praise — once told me that he never felt at ease in the pulpit without notes before him, because his people were accustomed to these, and would feel, in the absence of them, that his preparation had been incomplete, and that the service was insufficient. A very eminent clergyman of this city, who sustains important relations to this institution, has told me the same thing, in substance, of himself, within a few weeks. With all his culture, all his power, and all the prestige given by many honorable years of Christian service, — though speaking on the platform with ease, elegance, and continual success, — it has always been an awkward thing to him to stand in his pulpit without a manuscript. Even Dr. Bethune — wonderfully free, versatile, engaging, impressive, as he was, in almost all forms of public address — I think invariably took notes with him to the pulpit: that even if he did not use them he might have them on the desk, open before him.

The sympathies of a congregation are extremely swift and subtle. If a few are surprised, disappointed, restless, when they see you in the pulpit without a manuscript, if they turn away as careless of your words and expectant of failure, the feeling will propagate itself rapidly and far; and to speak freely, with self-possession, in the face of such indifference or distrust, will be very difficult. It is like trying to laugh aloud in a vacuum. You want the interest on the part of your people, to stimulate your powers. You want the quickening warmth of sympathy. One does see, I know, roses and pinks blooming on the terraces around Genoa in the month of December, with ice near them, half-an-inch thick, on the basins of fountains. But that has always seemed to me an almost unaccountable physical fact. And certainly the mind will not germinate and bloom in an atmosphere full of icy indifference. The spirit of the speaker will inevitably be affected by the doubt and disappointment which encircle and chill him. He will begin to hesitate, because he is thus hindered; and very likely will begin, before many minutes, to feel his heart beat, and his unsustained head reel and swim. When that comes to pass he had better sit down.

It is far better to avoid such manacles and miseries at the very start, by putting yourself on your feet and at ease with your people at once, through their thorough understanding of what you mean to do, and of the reasons which move you to do it. Let it be distinctly understood by them that at one of the services, at least — the morning, I think, being usually the better — you will preach without notes. Then you won't have to contend, at any rate, against their disappointment. The difficulties you meet afterward will be only intrinsic, and not adventitious. And that of itself will be a great gain.

And FOURTHLY: *Discharge your mind of the sermon when once you have preached it;* so keeping the mind free and open for other subjects succeeding that one.

I cannot give you any rule by which to do this. I only know that it can be done, though it is not easy; that the habit of doing it can be formed, like the habit of dining at a certain hour, or of walking at a certain pace, or like any other habit which we make for ourselves. And I know that it is indispensable to one who would speak energetically, usefully, without help from his notes.

The lawyer does it, all the time. All sorts of

cases come successively before him, and each, in its turn, fully occupies his mind: cases of insurance; cases involving felony — murder, theft, forgery, barratry, libel, or what not; cases of patent-rights; cases involving the title to lands; horse-cases, perhaps. While he is arguing one, his thoughts are full of it. The next eliminates it wholly from his mind; and the one is forgotten when the other is before him.

A minister must learn to do much the same thing. It is not easy, as I said. I used to be more embarrassed at this point than at almost any other. But I found that one great secret of success in doing what was needed was to take a second subject very different from the first: then the expulsive power of the new subject, occupying the thoughts, freed them from embarrassing reminiscences of the other. If you have preached on a theme of doctrine, for example, in the morning, take some point of Christian practice for your theme in the evening. If one discourse is preceptive and hortatory, let another be narrative, in its structure. If one is closely argumentative, let the next be a careful yet free exposition of a parable or a psalm. So you will find that the mind releases itself from the one subject, by taking another entirely distinct; its natural resilience is helped and stimulated, and you cease to be weighted with your previous processes.

In this way, or some other, you must secure the result which I indicate. Otherwise, you will be all the while in danger of repeating preceding trains of thought, of applying the intellectual methods proper to one subject to another widely different, and of wholly failing to widen and enrich your mind. You will be likely, even, to get by degrees a set of pet subjects, of recurring phrases, and of familiar illustrations; and to feel yourself, and to make your people feel as well, that your mind is becoming narrow and unproductive through your method of preaching. Applying the same general modes of treatment to all sorts of subjects, and getting the subjects themselves continually mixed and tangled in your thoughts, your whole force will dwindle.

The "evangelists" of forty years ago were accustomed to get a set of sermons — enough perhaps for four or six weeks of daily preaching — and then to go from place to place delivering these. They investigated no fresh subjects, but repeated the discourses which they had prepared, over and over. The result was that the first impression made by them was always vivid and energetic; but they became less convincing and powerful as they went on, till at last their minds were as dull and flameless as a burnt cinder. They were some of them powerful men, in their day: but their very names are now almost forgotten; and those who continued in that form of service left no more impression of themselves on the religious thought of the country, or on its theological literature, than a bird's wing leaves on the air.

You *must* keep the mind fresh and hospitable for new subjects, keep it all the time alert and advancing, if you are to preach without a manuscript with any success. Each sermon must have its own vitality, and stand apart from every other. You must be as free in discussing each succeeding subject as you were in treating the one before; and in order to this the sermon once preached must be thereafter wholly and swiftly discharged from the thoughts.

There is a certain disadvantage here, or what may appear such, in preaching without notes. It relates to exchanges of your pulpit for others. When one writes his sermons, an exchange of pulpits means a week's or a half-week's less work in the year. The sermons already prepared are at hand; and the principal duty is to read them. On the other hand, one often finds quite as much difficulty, I do not know but more, in re-charging the mind with a previous sermon, to be preached in exchange, than he did in preparing it at the outset, if there exists no manuscript of it. To re-absorb is harder than to produce. It is more difficult in preaching it the second time to keep the recollective force of the mind in abeyance, and to let the constructive, creative forces freely work. I confess that to this day an exchange of pulpits rather dismays me. I should always prefer to stay at home.

However, one can acquire more and more facility in doing this; and he will always find that the more vitally, thoroughly, he fills his mind with the subject which he treats, at home or abroad, the more effective he is in preaching. So I don't think that there is here any real disadvantage, except to the lazy. I verily believe, Young Gentlemen, that the kingdom of God advances more on spoken words than it does on essays written and read; on words, that is, in which the present feeling and thought of the teaching mind break into natural and forceful expression. There is always reward, therefore, as well as work, in fitting oneself for performing this office; and the work itself should only be to us an incentive.

FIFTHLY: *Never be discouraged by what seems to you, perhaps to others, comparative failure.*

Such failure occurs everywhere. Lawyers lose cases, and physicians lose patients. Even editors, it is said, sometimes write articles that are not absolutely brilliant and powerful, up to the line of their highest capacity. The painter fails to secure a good portrait, though he has such a subject as Gerrit Smith or Charlotte Cushman. The architect's mind gets into a cramp, and he can do nothing in planning the building to his own satisfaction. Men who write sermons fail, at times, as well as those who preach without notes. They write in a languid and inert state; they quarrel with the discourses while they preach them; very likely they burn them when they are done. My father once burned four hundred at a flash; and I always honored him for it.

So don't be discouraged, as if it were a thing that never happened to any other sort of workman if you fail in your effort when treating a subject without a manuscript. It is not impossible that what seems to you failure may appear quite otherwise to your people. They may be most impressed by that with which you are most discontented. The train of thought which had interested your mind, but which would not come back while you were speaking, would have been too subtle and refined for your hearers. The commoner thoughts which you were obliged to substitute for it reached some of them more effectively. The fine processes, in which you had rejoiced but which you forgot, would have been too delicate. The bolder broad-axe style of treatment, to which you resorted but of which you were ashamed, did better service. The most numerous and inspiriting echoes often come back from what you esteemed your poorest work: and you find to your surprise that hearts were comforted, despondencies were dispelled, faltering wills received fresh impulse, from the very sermon which to you appeared a perfect failure.*

* Note VII.

At any rate remember this: that your business is to *do the best you can* in the preaching of the Gospel, every time you stand in the pulpit; and if you are conscious that you have done that, before the sermon and in the sermon, then let that suffice. If you feel that you have failed of the success which you hoped for, if disparaging remarks come back to you from others, be never discouraged; and certainly never get morbid about it. "In your patience possess ye your souls:" if your Greek Professor will allow the translation, 'by your endurance, get full possession, and perfect mastery, of your own souls.' That is the first step toward getting an equal mastery over others. "Quit you like men; be strong." "Forgetting the things which are behind, reach forth" — stretch forth, bending forward, as the racer toward the goal — unto those which are before.

Remember the pains men take to train themselves in other and lower departments of effort, and be ashamed if you are not willing to give to this grandest office on earth the labor and self-discipline which are needed for success in it. I see the athlete, the gymnast, the rope-walker, the man who is to swing upon the trapeze, developing each muscle, giving every nerve its fitting training, for the feats they accomplish, until the results are simply amazing; I remember the tough pugilistic expression which Paul employs, "I keep under the body," *ὑπωπιάζω*, — I beat it black and blue, if needful — and bring it to subjection; and then I think with shame how few and slight, in comparison are the efforts which we make for success in our calling. I remember a sword-dance which I once saw at Würzburg, in Bavaria, performed by some Arabian gymnasts, leaping over and among the gleaming, sharp, and cruel blades which would have instantly drunk the life from you or me, but amid which they lightly sprang and danced, as if they had been stalks of thistle; and I say to myself, and repeat it to you, How ready should we be to give ourselves a training for our work as much more exact and thorough than theirs as our work is more important!' *

If you do this, in the final result you will not fail; and if, in your preliminary efforts, you now and then do fail, be never discouraged. Make the failure a reason for more intense succeeding effort; a wing, not a weight; a spur, to stimulate to fresh endeavor, and not a stiletto, to stab out the life!

But, FINALLY, Gentlemen: *Do no violence to your own nature;* — and if you find, after sufficient conscientious trial, that you can do more useful service with the pen than without it, then use the pen, without reluctance, without reserve, and be thankful that you have it.

There are some men, no doubt, who can never acquire complete self-possession in presence of an audience, so as to be at ease and in vigor when addressing large numbers face to face. They are fewer, I am confident, than is commonly supposed. But there are some such; who can

* Note VIII.

hardly, at any rate, prepare themselves for this office without such a martyrdom as they are not called to; while the same men may be swift, bold, powerful, with the pen, and in reading their writings may be very effective. It would be a wanton waste of time, if not indeed a sin against nature, for such men to give up their notes in the pulpit. They ought to use them, and to be grateful to God for this means of usefulness. The pen is a prodigious power in the world; an invincible moral and social force; a real lever to lift the race forward. It has blessed all times, since man first discovered the use of the alphabet. God Himself has put honor upon it, in writing His law on tables of stone, and not merely speaking it in articulate tones. He has honored it in the gospels, preserving by it the words of His Son. Any man should be glad and proud to use it, for Him from whom the power comes.

I have never believed it the best plan for all ministers to preach without notes. I only think it better for some. And my remarks, now and hereafter, are intended only for those among you who think that it may be better for them. If you think so, I shall be delighted to say any word that may help you in your effort. For really I think the work you contemplate as great a work as ever is given to men on earth : to bring Divine truths, with earnest utterance, to human souls. Never look upon your congregation as so many 'cabbage-heads,' as some one has inconsiderately said, but always look on them as immortal intelligences, each one of whom shall live forever! and then bring all the power you can to urge them to righteousness, through thoughtful, fervent, inspiring speech. It is the noblest of human errands. Whether, therefore, you do your work with notes or without them, do it courageously, earnestly, with devotion; with a glad sense of the greatness of it, and a full consecration of every force and faculty to it.

If I might change one letter in a precept of St. Paul, I should say: " One man esteemeth one way above another; another man esteemeth every way alike. Let every man be fully persuaded in his own mind." And whichever way you finally select, strive always to be able to say: "Whether we live, we live unto the Lord; and whether we die, we die unto the Lord. Whether we live, therefore, or die, we are the Lord's."

Working for the Master in this high spirit, the work which you do will be always noble; and the reward which comes after it will be sure, and immortal!

SECOND LECTURE.

Mr. President: Young Gentlemen: —

I am very happy to meet you here again, — the more so, as an hour ago, while I was drifting about the Bay, I thought it very doubtful if I should be able to meet you at all. The fact is that you people who live on the wrong side of the East River are apt to get *i*solated — if you will pardon the pronunciation — in such weather as this; and we, who live where we ought to, find it hard work to get to you.

I ought perhaps, to add, before beginning upon my subject this afternoon, that I have been occupied, to-day, before leaving home, with some of those sad and exacting duties of which every minister meets so many, which for the time wholly occupy his mind, and draw largely upon his sympathies; so that you may find me, I fear, even less prepared than I should otherwise have been to speak to you on the theme before us. I shall trust to your kindness to excuse the defects which you may observe.

I am again surprised by finding present not only the students of this institution, to whom, as being younger than myself, I had thought it possible that I might say something which should be of more or less service in their coming work, but also these distinguished men — Professors, Pastors, Secretaries, Editors, Presidents of Colleges, Lawyers, Teachers, and eminent Merchants, whom I have not come prepared to address. I can only say that when I am invited to breakfast or lunch I do not go dressed for an evening dinner-party; and when I am asked to speak to students, who may not know even as much as myself, I do not prepare myself to speak to others who know much more. I long ago found cut that when a Committee ask one to 'make a few remarks,' what they mean is 'an address of half-an-hour.' But I certainly thought that I was perfectly safe in literally accepting the kind invitation of these Professors and Doctors of Divinity, and coming to speak to students only.

At any rate, I shall stick to the programme, and "talk," as I intended, without attempting any studied and elaborate address, suitable for these gentlemen accomplished in their professions.

Let me say, still further, that after my rapid talk of last week I was pursued with the fear that I must have seemed egotistical in it; as if I quite over-estimated the consequence of whatever experience I have had, in the matter of preaching without my notes. I hope, however, that you did me the justice to look at the thing from my point of view, and to recognize the fact that I said what I did only because it seemed inevitable, as laying the basis for my subsequent suggestions; and, also, as illustrating the fact that there was nothing whatever exceptional in my case; that the change in my method was not a sudden one; that whatever I have done in this direction has been only the result of continuous effort, and that anybody else who wishes to do it, and is willing to work for it, can do as much: — some of you, I am sure, can do much more, as I sincerely hope that you will.

Now for what I have principally to say to-day.

After the preliminary suggestions which I made last week I propose to present to you certain specific conditions of success — or what I esteem such — in the work of preaching without one's notes. First I shall speak of those which are especially physical and mental, and afterward of those which are moral and spiritual. Those of the latter class I shall hope to present next week. Of those of the former class I shall speak to-day. Some of them are essential; all of them are important; and in the absence of any one of them, the highest success can hardly, I think, be ever realized.

Before proceeding to consider them, however, one by one, let me say in general, as preliminary to every thing which is to follow, that I assume, as an essential pre-requisite to all such success, *a serious, devout, intelligent, inspiring conviction of the Divine origin and authority of the Gospel, and of its transcendent importance to men.* — This is a fundamental condition, indispensable to every thing else; and without it no instruction or rule that I know of can be of real service to any preacher.

Of course, this is not merely a condition to success in preaching without a manuscript. It is a condition to such success in preaching in any way, either with notes or without them. No man can hope to accomplish results, permanent and fruitful, in the work of the ministry, unless this conviction is in his mind, radicated there, ruling over his thoughts, inspiring him to constant endeavors, and kindling in him a constant enthusiasm.

It is difficult to see, indeed, why a man without this should ever enter the ministry at all, as long as bread and meat can be won in other reputable ways. His work must be an immensely hard one, and its pull upon him must be very exhausting. For a man in preaching has not only to give sermons, grammatically composed, but in order to render effective service he must speak, or must seem to speak, from the heart; and if one has not the love of the Gospel enthroned in his heart the work must draw with prodigious force on all his nature, mental and moral, while the reward for it can never be large. Such a one will almost certainly be soon introducing some novelty of doctrine, to refresh his mind with what enlists his conviction, or what at least is attractive to his thought. He will tend more and more to become a mere teacher of natural ethics, or of social philosophy; and after a while will be likely to leave the ministry altogether.

A man *must* have faith in God's authorship of the Gospel, and in its importance to man's well-being, in order to impulse and success in proclaiming it. This is necessary, if for no other reason, that he himself may understand his proper function and errand in the world;

that he may recognize himself as essentially a herald — *κῆρυξ, κηρύσσω* — proclaiming the glad tidings of God to mankind. He is not sent to be an ingenious and eloquent sophist, inventing theories of his own, or accepting the theories invented by others. He is to bring to men the wisdom which God has first revealed to him in His word, — accepting, pondering, absorbing that, in his own mind, and then declaring it vividly to others, through character and through speech. So his office becomes a grand one: unique, in fact, among the offices accomplished by man. So he is brought into intimate communion with the mind of the Most High. Strength of purpose, expectation of success, and a serene fearlessness, become the very prerogatives of his office, when he stands to represent the King of the world, in uttering His messages to the men of the world.*

The same conviction of the Divine origin and authority of the Gospel, and of its infinite im-

* Note IX.

portance to man, is needed to help one in meditating his subject, as well as in presenting it. It will quicken him in his study, as well as in the pulpit, if he understands that his business is, in investigating the word, to ascertain what the thought of God is, as therein set forth, and then to present it — while gathering around it all the lights of reflection and scholarship, that he may make it most evident and lucent, and in its presentation most commanding and attractive. This will lift him to higher levels of thought, and lead him out into widest ranges of inquiry and study. It will draw forth and stimulate each power within him, that he may apprehend what the Author of the Gospel would have him speak, and may speak it in a manner most pertinent and persuasive.

It will kindle his enthusiasm, and help him in even the delivery of his message, making him courageous, and setting him free from all bondage to circumstances, however embarrassing these may be. We hear a great deal said, in these days, about awkward pulpits; how high they often are, how narrow, how restraining. There is something in it. They are often very awkward; and I criticise no one who prefers a plain desk, on an open stage, to one of those embattled boxes into which a minister sometimes is put. I would certainly rather myself stand here, and speak to you from this platform, than attempt to do it from the pulpit behind me: though we all have seen those which were far worse than that.

I remember, years ago, when I was settled at Brookline, an excellent minister, now deceased, who was then a somewhat distinguished man, came one Sunday to preach for me. He was shorter than I was, and I therefore thought that he might like the desk lowered, on which the sermon was to lie, and suggested this to him. But he said, No; and it remained as it was. I found afterward that he was short-sighted, and yet preferred to use no glasses: so the manuscript must be brought as closely as possible to his eye. Instead of lowering the desk, he raised it still higher, as high as it would go. He then closed the Bible, which had lain open upon it. He placed a hymn-book on that; another hymn-book on that; a pile of sermons, a dozen I should think, on the top of that; and then the sermon which he was to read, surmounting the whole. When the whole structure had been erected, he was left standing behind it, and just able to look over it, while the congregation could see almost nothing of him but the top of his head. Then he read his text, as his custom was, without first naming its place in the Scripture; and the text proved to be: "Ye shall see greater things than these!" It was a serious service, and a devout congregation; but the smile that rippled round the room, if not quite as loud as this of yours, was quite as instant and universal.

Any man may be pardoned for not desiring a breast-work like that, between him and the people. But if one is penetrated, is essentially imbued, with the thorough conviction that the message which he brings is a message from God, and that it is vital to man's well-being, it will not make much difference to him where he preaches. Even such a barricade could not hinder his utterance. He will preach on the swinging deck of a ship, so long as he is not sea-sick ; on the stump, around which the pioneers gather ; on a box, at the street-corner ; if need be, from the 'Devil's pulpit,' on Monument Mountain. He will be at home in whatever circumstances, if this conviction really fills him, that the word which he preaches is God's word to man.*

Some one has said that "no faculty of the mind is weak which has heart in it." Certainly it is true that no faculty is strong which has not heart in it; and whoever addresses men has to learn the lesson. If one is to speak on Sanitary Reform, he needs the underlying sense of the greatness of the interest of public health, and of the importance of the measures which he advo-

* Note X.

cates to the maintenance of that health. If he is to speak for the maintenance and the furtherance of International Peace, he needs to feel how vast are its blessings, and how tremendous the miseries and sins which it displaces, the moral decadence which it will arrest.

So, and still more, if he speaks of the Gospel, he must feel how glorious that is in itself, and how adapted to man's vast need. This must be the undertone of every sermon; like the golden ground on which the angels of Fra Angelico walk and worship. The conviction of it must be as a sun-gleam, smiting his mind, and quickening to activity all its beauty and all its force. If he has not this, his thought will inevitably be obscure, his feeling dull, his utterance wanting in the elements of power. A deist, a fatalist, a materialist, a sceptic of whatever sort, undertaking as a business to preach the Gospel, will inevitably be like a blind man discoursing on the splendors of light, and the charming and delicate interplay of colors; or like a deaf man, describing oratorios. Every one who loves the Gospel will see that he is speaking theoretically, in the way of imitation, from report of others, and not from real and rich experience. So his words will want fire. They will stir no emotion, and touch no heart. They will be like a smile, in which the lips laugh, while the rest of the face is harsh and sullen.

In order then that a man may have this conviction, pervading his mind — that the Gospel is God's word to the world, and that he is but a herald sent to proclaim it — that he may enter into this high enthusiasm, and keep his spirit glowing with it, he should meditate much on the facts which prove God's authorship of the Scripture: on the amazing unity of the Bible; on its majesty, surpassing all reach of man's thought; on the holiness of its law — a holiness against which man's will rebels, and which could not have sprung from the nature that resists it; on its perfect adaptation to human wants, its power to soothe, to inspire, and to purify, the peace it gives to the penitent heart, the hope it quickens in darkest hours, the tranquil courage it gives in death. Keep your minds under the manifold proofs of God's authorship of the Gospel — proofs which in the aggregate amount to demonstration — till the soul is glowing and incandescent with this conviction: that you in proclaiming this to men are speaking to them the thoughts of the Almighty. The constant inspiring force of this will exalt your whole ministry.

Now for the specific conditions of which I am to speak, which are important to any man's success who would preach this Gospel without aid from notes.

The FIRST which I mention is: *Physical vigor, kept at its highest attainable point.*

You will think that I begin a good way back, and so I do; but this is the under-pinning of every thing else, and it must be treated as first in order.

Of course we know that the healthiest men

are by no means always the most intellectual. It is not necessary that a man should be trained like a prize-fighter, in active service, to be a good preacher. But the intellectual man is always then in the best condition for effective, vigorous, sustained mental effort, when his physical vigor is most nearly at its height. It is not necessary to go into any argument to show this, or carefully to develop the subtle relations between physiology and psychology. Experience proves it.

Every student knows, for example, how easy and swift mental processes are on some days, which on others are tardy and difficult; because in the one case the mind takes vigor from the body, and the thoughts go forth refreshed by its health, while in the other case there seems to be a mist on the brain, from some perturbed state of the physical system, or the invisible spiritual muscle which holds the mind to a strict and searching investigation of subjects has been silently relaxed. A clear, crisp morning-air:

how it sets the very soul in a glow, on a day like this! After a brisk and breezy walk, after a swim beyond the breakers, after a rapid horseback ride — it is astonishing, the swift change which is wrought, of mental renewal; how subjects clear up, and faculty is freshened, and we are ready for any work. After sound and sufficient sleep, we wake in the morning prepared for efforts which in the weariness of the preceding evening had been simply impossible. Reading, conversation, public discourse — any thing is then possible, the refreshed body lending enterprise to the mind.

This emphasizes the rule that we *must* maintain, as far as we can, full health of body, if we would discourse to men on the themes of the Gospel, without help from a manuscript, with any success. Such health is the bed-plate, on which the whole mental machinery must rest and work. If this be cracked, or displaced, all the mechanism that stands on it will be jarred and disturbed, and made ineffective. You must work the ship after that, if you work it at all, with the donkey-engine.

Such health, indeed, is particularly necessary to the rapid, robust, effective working of those special faculties which are always most needed in public speech. The judgment, the will, the creative imagination, — the power of rapidly originating thought, and as rapidly combining it in relations with others, — the power of expressing it freely and with facility, and so of setting forth the subjects which are treated in energetic and perspicuous speech: these are the powers which the preacher requires, if he is to speak without aid from his notes. And these are the powers which depend most eminently on fulness of health as their condition.

It may not be so with some other faculties. The fancy, for instance, may sometimes act most rapidly and brilliantly, in connection with morbid physical conditions; as is shown in not a few poets and artists, perhaps in some preachers. The memory will sometimes show abnormal activity when the brain is in any thing but a healthful condition; and the emotional nature is undoubtedly more excitable — though its power of propagating emotion in others is not, I think, in like measure increased — when the body is suffering from a diseased sensibility.

So it may be with still other faculties. But the general and harmonious intellectual vigor, whereby one conceives subjects clearly and fully, analyzes them rapidly, sets them forth with exactness in an orderly presentation, and urges them powerfully on those who listen — this requires opulence of health; a sustained and abounding physical vigor. In the absence of this, the power will decline. If the mind still works energetically at all, it will do so only by jerks, and in spasms, not continuously; will do it with particular faculties, not with the consentaneous and coöperating energy of all its powers, working together for a noble result. It may surprise men, still; but it hardly by possibility will sway and inspire them.

A conscious and abundant physical vigor is necessary, even, to a fit and impressive delivery of one's thoughts. The weak man is apt to screech in his utterance, and now and then to explode in his tones; while the strong man speaks easily, naturally, without any push of his voice by the will. His is a power which comes from within, and which manifests itself as freely and steadily as the power that moves the levers of machinery.

Indeed, such sound physical health is, directly, a positive power to the speaker. It has almost a moral force in it. It represents a complete development of manhood in him; and it carries men forward, with immediate impulse, on the efflux of its force. Webster is the typical illustration of this among American speakers. The vast mass of the man made his words impressive. As a farmer said of him, after hearing one of his brief addresses: "He didn't say very much, but every word that he did say weighed a pound." He carried men's minds, and overwhelmingly pressed his thought upon them, with the immense current of his physical energy. Once in a famous case at Northampton — known to the lawyers as the "Smith-will case" — where a large property was involved, Mr. Webster was employed for the maintenance of the will, and Mr. Choate was his antagonist. At one point in the progress of the trial Mr. Choate quoted a *dictum*, — from Lord Camden, I think it was, — to the effect that a witness to the execution of an instrument must be competent not only to certify to the fact of the manual signature of the person by whom the paper was executed, but also to judge of his mental soundness at the time of his signing it. Mr. Choate cited this, in impeachment of one of the witnesses to the will. Mr. Webster could not avoid meeting it. When he came to it he said, in substance, as I have been told: 'My learned friend has quoted from Lord Camden, to this effect' — (repeating the *dictum*). 'Gentlemen, this means that when you call in one of your farm-hands to witness your signature to a conveyance or a mortgage, he is not merely to see you write your name, but he is to be able to look into your mind, and see if that is sound and discreet! Lord Camden says that.' Then up went his head, and out went his chest: 'Daniel Webster says THAT'S NONSENSE.' And so it was, for that jury at any rate.

We cannot certainly be Daniel Websters, either physically or mentally. But we may attain our fair share of physical vigor, and gain the force which comes with that. It is especially needful, I think, to the minister. An impression sometimes prevails among people that religion is good for dyspeptics and invalids, for nervous people, and for women; but that it does not suit well with a body full of spirit and health. They are apt to expect to find in the minister a debilitated student, who does not know much of what real and vigorous manhood means. His words are for persons like himself; and not for hale men, in an out-door life. A full development of vital force, a robust and athletic habit of body, if he can gain it, is the very best answer to such an idea. Therefore, if for this reason only, it is a Christian duty to gain it, and to keep our merely physical force at the highest point.

When I was ordained I was in somewhat delicate health, not long recovered from a serious sickness, thinner and paler than I have since been. The "Charge" was given to me by a most excellent man, a friend of my father for many years, a friend of my own from my boyhood up, to whom I was attached by many tender and grateful ties, and whom I had every reason to revere. He was a man of very full and florid habit, who had not seen his knees, as they say, for twenty years; and as he stood speaking on the platform, while I stood listening beneath, the contrast between us was undoubtedly striking. It was emphasized, perhaps, to some of the congregation, when looking at me with tears in his eyes, he said very earnestly:

"My young brother, I charge you, Keep under the body!"

It did seem rather absurd at the time, as an address from him to me; but it was nevertheless a sound, wholesome, apostolic charge. He meant what he said; and I should repeat it on every occasion when such a service was committed to me. I repeat it to myself to-day, and repeat it to you: "Keep under the body." Only be careful to give the precept its proper meaning, and to obey it in the right sense. Keep under the body, as the rider keeps his horse beneath him; as the sailor keeps the deck; as the builder keeps ladder and scaffolding beneath him. Keep it in constant subjection to the mind. Keep it under, that the whole intellectual force may securely rest and rise upon it; that it may be not an opponent of the spirit, but its continual supporter and minister.

In order to this, avail yourselves of all the means which experience suggests, your own or others'. Leave no means untried, that are apt to the end. Use good, simple, wholesome food, and plenty of it. Find out for yourselves what food suits you best, and govern yourselves accordingly, without reference to the theories of other people about it. Take exercise as you need it, and physical recreation. Get plenty of sleep, and as early as you can. The 'beauty-sleep' of the mind comes generally before midnight. Do your work in the day-time, in the sunshine, if possible; under the light which God has given, and not in an artificial blaze. Enjoy the intervals of rest and relaxation, as you have opportunity, and as you find need.*

Use every help, which experience indicates as reasonable and right, to secure the condition, and maintain the condition, of full normal physical vigor; and remember that you are responsible to no man for that which you do in order to this supreme result. You are responsible to the Son of God, and to God Himself — who has given you the body as the instrument

* Note XI.

through which the mind is to work; who requires you to keep it continually attuned for effective continuous service. So nourish and train it, to the highest point of strength and vigor attainable by you ; and whenever you speak without a manuscript you will feel the effect. Force, buoyancy, elasticity, vigor, will come to the mind from the sound and energetic physical force which underlies and sustains it.

And this leads me to say, SECONDLY : Be very sure to *keep your mind in a state of habitual activity, alertness, energy ;* — so that it will be ready to grasp subjects strongly, and to handle them with easy and effectual force; so that thoughts shall come to you rapidly when you speak, and your freedom in uttering them be proportioned to the rapidity with which they are suggested.

Keep the mind up to its highest point. Of course we all know the immense differences that appear in it, at different times, in regard to that dynamic force by which it seizes a subject presented, opens it rapidly in its parts and relations, and sets it forth clearly for others to consider. Sometimes it seems impossible to accomplish what at other times is easy. Things are dim and obscure to us on one day, which on another are manifest, vivid. The whole atmosphere seems changed.

A man going up Mount Washington sometimes finds at the top only a cloudy or stormy darkness, through which the sight does not pass at all. The whole peak welters in waves of fog. On another day — called by those who live there 'bright' — the air is full of a shimmering haze, in which the light-rays seem inter-twisted and tangled together, so that no eye can fairly pierce the glittering mist. It sees only summits of the neighboring mountains, surging around the central crest. But at last there comes a resplendent day, when through the clear transpicuous air you look afar. Your vision has found its perfect medium. You see the green meadows of Conway lying almost at your feet, with the Saco winding through; and sixty miles away, as the bird flies, you look into the harbor of Portland, and perhaps see beyond it the flash of sails out on the sea.

There are states of the mind which correspond with these changes, and of which they are the physical parallel. There come to us sometimes high, luminous moments, of vision and intuition, when we see at a glance what before had been hidden, and realms of thought are instantly opened; when a moment will do for us, what previous hours had failed to accomplish. Then subjects instantaneously take form, discourses shape themselves in our thoughts, and both outline and detail are conceived at once with perfect vividness.*

This story is told of an eminent living clergyman: I will not vouch for it, in all its particulars, but in its main features I have the assurance that it is authentic. He was walking one evening to a church at New Haven, at

* Note XII.

which he was to preach, with a young lady, at whose home perhaps he had been entertained. She said to him on the way: "Dr. C—, is it true, as I have heard, that you sometimes do not select your text till you have gone into the pulpit?" "Yes," he said, "it is sometimes true; and I wish you would give me a text for this evening, for really I have not yet decided on what to preach." "I would if I could," she said; "but I can't think of any text at this moment, unless it be: 'The Lord spake unto Moses and unto Aaron, saying.'" "Excellent!" said he. "It is precisely what I want: I shall preach upon that." And he did. It would puzzle us, perhaps, to discern at a glance what he saw in it. But it was one of the grandest subjects that can be given to any preacher, that can be considered by any man. It was the vast subject of the Divine Revelation. It opened to him, all at a flash, like a bright broad landscape seen through a crevice.

Man's need of such a Revelation from above,

and his constant tendency to sink into deeper darkness without it; the fair expectation, from God's wisdom and goodness, that He will give it; the different modes in which it is shown by Scripture to have been given — by oral utterance, by written words, by ecstatic visions and dreams, by prophetic inspiration, by the coming of the Son of God Himself, who shows to the world the very mind of God, as well as utters His separate thoughts, at last by the advent of the Holy Ghost, teaching the evangelists and the apostles; then by all these, combined in one Bible, a book for all ages, a book for the world, a book to be interpreted to the studious reader by the same Divine Spirit from which its inspiration came: — this was the substance of the sermon. Then followed the lessons: of the grace of God, in giving this to man, and preserving it in the world; of the duty and privilege of attending to it; of the wickedness of substituting any thing for it — either Reason, or the Church; of the glory of the state in which even this Revelation will be needed no more, since we shall see God face to face.

The whole discourse — as represented to me — was compact, complete, powerful, from the outset on; because it was fashioned by a mind in this high, fervid, luminous state of which I have spoken. It was precisely adapted, also, to a semi-sceptical state of mind at that time prevailing in the college, of which he was aware; and so it was every way timely and effective.

Well, of course, this is an extraordinary instance; as the mental state expressed in it was extraordinary. But I suspect that every man who is much accustomed to speaking without manuscript has met something like it in his experience. The mind now and then comes into a state in which any suggestion, any occurrence, will evoke great fulness and force of thought. It is then like a battery fully charged. It does not take a 64 pounder to draw out the flash from such a battery. A knitting-needle will do it; the smallest bit of broken wire. And nothing is easier than to preach in that mood. Any text that is touched will set in motion trains of thought, to be instantly elaborated, and ready for instant presentation.

But this state of mind cannot be extemporized. The will can no more create it at pleasure than it can make us three inches taller. It will always be found, when it has come, to have had deep vital roots beneath it. How then can we gain it? and keep the mind in this best condition for grandest service? The means are many. I can mention only one or two.

Reading, intently, and rapidly, is one of them. There is great virtue in rapid reading, when it is also attentive and studious. Ours is apt, I think, to be too lazy, indolent, self-indulgent. We read, and hardly know sometimes whether we are reading or dozing.* Reading rapidly, as well as attentively, gives pace to the mind, a general celerity to the whole mental movement. It trains the intellectual force to just that sure

* Note XIII.

and vigorous quick-step which one always wants in speaking to men, with an earnest conviction, but without any notes. There is great benefit, therefore, in such reading; and the impulse and stimulus which one carries away from it are of more importance than many minor particulars of knowledge.

Read widely, too; history, science, philosophy, poetry, works on law, works on art, as well as discussions in metaphysics. Do not read too exclusively in theology. The man who confines himself wholly to that develops only a part of his mind; keeps only a certain set of faculties in exercise and training. He is apt to get an eye like a microscopic lens, fine in its distinctions, not wide in its range. What the minister needs, who would speak to men effectively, is the widest development. He should keep his mind, therefore, in quickening contact with other minds, in many and various departments of thought. Only eschew fiction; or use it, if at all, in great moderation. As a general thing, it doesn't help. It rather relaxes and ungirds the mind; acts as a laxative, or an anæsthetic, rather than as a real invigorant.

I do not know that I should go so far as to insist on your following precisely the example of an excellent friend of mine, who once read David Copperfield, when he had a tough toothache, and who afterward said to the gentleman who had furnished it that he did not know whether he had done right or not, but certainly he had not read any other work of fiction for twenty years; not since he read Bunyan's Holy War! But I should say, read it very little; in vacation, if at all, or in time of recreation, and not when you are actively at work. And when you read, read only the masters, — Thackeray, Dickens, Bulwer, Scott, and the like; and let the great herd of writers of stories go their way. They bring no profit. Keep the mind braced — that is the rule — by contact with large and disciplinary subjects, as treated by vigorous and liberal minds; and accustom yourselves to a swift and thorough redaction of subjects as you read. But do not read to the point of weariness. Absorb and assimilate as much as you can, but never undertake to carry the burden of multitudes of things to be afterward remembered. The force is what you want, rather than the load.*

Conversation, too, with equal minds, is of immense and constant service in refreshing the mind, and replenishing it with active force. Indeed, conversation, if practised as it ought to be, as a commerce of thought between responsive and interchanging minds, is an invaluable aid toward gaining the art of easy and self-possessed public speech. I do not think we have as much of it as we ought; or that it holds the place which it should in our plans of life, as a real educational force. It is much the same exercise, if you analyze it, with public speaking. Of course it is not the same altogether. In public speech your utterance of thought is more prolonged: it

* Note XIV.

is monologue, not dialogue. You miss the help which comes from interjected remarks or replies; and you are not so immediately conscious of the sympathy or the collision of the adjacent minds. Still, conversation is much the same form of mental activity; and it always helps the public speaker. It trains the mind to think rapidly, and to formulate thought with facility and success; and each sense of such success, which is gained in conversation, will give one more confidence when he stands before an audience.

Instead of talking to ten persons, you are there to talk to five hundred; but the one exercise has helped for the other, as singing in a parlor helps to sing in a choir, or as shooting with an air-gun, at ten paces, helps one to shoot straight with a rifle, at a hundred. One who is silent, secluded, all the week, without contact with men, had better always read his sermons. He will be certainly timorous, and self-conscious, when Sunday comes; afraid of other minds, except as they speak to him through books. But one who has the opportunity, and uses it, of energetic and frank conversation, on important subjects, with equal minds, will be reïnforced by it, and will be sure to come to his pulpit more ripe and ready for his work, more confident of his power to utter thought without having written it.

Variety of work, too, assists this result. I mean, of course, variety of work within reasonable limits. I shouldn't advise you, when you come to be ministers, to undertake any wholly superfluous work like this of mine — giving lectures to young gentlemen who already have professors to tell them more than their heads can hold! But aside from such absurd excess, within reasonable limits, the more various a man's work is, the more likely he is to keep his mind in an animated, active, and forceful state. When some one spoke, you know, to Dr. Lyman Beecher of a man who 'had too many irons in the fire,' his reply was, 'Nonsense! let him put them all in: poker, tongs, shovel, and all. It never will hurt him.' The fact that he himself was always so ready for any work, which promised important Christian success, was in part the secret of that commanding and quickening power which he possessed so largely and so long. Variety of occupation sets the spirit in a glow. It relieves one faculty by exercising another. It keeps all forces alert and ready, and tends to make one ambi-dextrous.*

With this variety of work, this habit of conversation, this rapid and wide reading, one may at any rate keep his mind at as high a state of freshness and energy as is to him possible. And in that state it is easy to speak one's thought to others. Then the stimulus of the audience only further assists him. When he comes to his congregation, and sees the eager listening faces upturned toward his, perhaps sees the flush or the tear as he speaks, there is immense incentive in it. He may then reach points of vision and power impossible to be attained in the study. He may even reproduce,

* Note XV.

in a measure, the experience of the eloquent preacher in this city, not of our faith, who is said to have said that when he had reached a certain occasional pitch of intensity, in conviction and feeling, he had nothing more to do with the sermon than just to open and shut his jaws. 'There is a little fellow up there in the brain who does the rest; and where it all comes from I hardly know.'

Then the mind walks on its high places. It works automatically, and with sovereign force, without constraint or urgency of volition. The man himself is amazed at the rush with which both thought and utterance come. The reserved forces all break into play. Things are at hand, which had seemed inaccessible. Previous knowledge is as if transfigured. The whole spirit is full of energy, full of light. It rejoices to reveal itself, in action and in speech; and its words are instinct with brightness and power.

Such moods will only come of themselves. They cannot be summoned by an effort of will, any more than you can make a cold day warmer by heating the thermometer. But they come only to minds prepared for them, by such a discipline as I have suggested. And when they come, you have the sense, as at no other time, of doing your kingly errand in the world for One who is Himself speaking through you — through the mind which, in all its intensified powers, is subordinate to His! When a congregation has once felt the luxury and the exhilaration of such an experience they will never be content until it has been repeated.*

Then, THIRDLY: *Be careful that the plan of your sermon is simple, natural, progressive, easily mastered, and is thoroughly imbedded in your mind.* — This seems to me indispensable.

If there is any secret in regard to speaking freely without notes, which I have learned, it is simply this: that the recollective forces of the mind, which are in their nature subordinate and auxiliary, are to be kept strictly in abeyance —

* Note XVI.

not to be called on for any service — so that the spontaneous, suggestive, creative powers may have continual and unhindered play. Nothing, if possible, should be left to be recalled at the time of speaking, by a distinct act of memory. The more you try to recollect, the less effective your sermon will be. The more frequently you have to look backward, in the course of it, the less aggressive productive energy will remain in your mind; and it is this, if any thing, which is to win and to move the assembly.

It is indispensable, therefore, that the main plan of the sermon be from the start so plainly in view that it comes up of itself, as it is needed, and does not require to be pulled into sight with any effort. To this end, it must be simple, obvious, natural, so that it fixes itself in the mind; and must be clearly articulated in its parts. If possible, let it be so arranged that one point naturally leads to another, and, when the treatment of it is finished, leaves you in front of that which comes next. Then take up that, and treat it in its order, until, through that treatment, you reach the third, and find it inevitable to proceed to consider that. By such a progressive arrangement of thought you are yourself carried forward; your faculties have continual liberty; you are not forced to pause in the work of addressing yourself directly to the people.

Of course you may secure this in either one of a variety of ways.

You may get it, for example, by a strictly textual division of the subject, when the structure of your text admits of that. Take Paul's declaration, for example, in his epistle to the Romans: [viii. 28.] "And we know that all things work together for good to them that love God, to them who are the called according to his purpose." "We know:" what right had Paul to speak thus, with such supreme certainty? Because he had been assured of it by God, and had found it verified in his experience. We may rest on his knowledge, and make it ours. "All things:" all facts, and forces, and laws of the universe, from the smallest animalcule to the star Alcyone: what a measureless compass in this declaration! "Work:" nothing is inactive, all things, and all beings, under God's ordination, are in motion for effects. "Work together:" in harmony with each other, as all proceeding from one Divine mind, and moving in the development of one supreme plan. "Work together for good:" the beneficence of all in the final result; such as must be anticipated, since He from whom they start is good, and He cannot do otherwise than manifest His character in the ends toward which the universe tends. But it is for good "to them that love Him:" to those who are in union, by moral sympathy, with the Head of the creation, having been lifted and inspired to that sympathy by His inviting and quickening grace.

The text itself suggests the succession of the divisions, if you choose so to treat it; and each following word is the fulcrum of an argument.

And then the practical lessons come, just as

naturally: of comfort to those who are in trouble; of courage and enterprise to those who are trying to work for God; of assurance of hope, to those who are consciously allied to Him, through joyful and affectionate faith in His Son. — There is nothing here to be laboriously recalled. It presents itself, as fast as you want it; and you could not forget it, if you tried.

Or, you may reach the same result by a topical division of the subject, if you prefer that. Take, for example, another declaration of the same great Apostle, in his letter to the Colossians: [i. 14.] "In whom we have redemption through his blood, even the forgiveness of sins." — There is a consciousness of sin in every man; of omission, at least, if not of wrong-doing; of defect in virtue, if not of a fierce and virulent depravity. With this comes the conscious need of forgiveness, which is the inevitable correlative of the other, and will be apparent to all who are thoughtful. Is there any answer then, on the part of God to this need of ours? Several answers are current in the world, and challenge attention.

It is said, for example, that He never forgives; He cannot, in the nature of the case. Moral forces work as irresistibly, moral laws are as inexorable, as those which rule in the physical world. The man who breaks law must take the consequences. The morally poisoned cannot be helped. — This is the positivist, the deistical idea. It is a terrible response to our keen and tremulous sense of need.

Another is, that He forgives capriciously: those who have been born of good parents; those who have lived in Christian society; who have had a fortunate mental constitution; who have been influential; who have not done any thing flagrantly bad; — such are forgiven, though no change of character is manifest in them. This is an answer, if possible, still more terrible than the other; since the man unforgiven is discriminated against, in favor of one who had a better opportunity. That *cannot* be admitted.

A third answer is, that He forgives universally, without reference to circumstances, without distinction of character, because He is kind: and this is the worst conception of all.— For by it all moral law is annulled, and chaos comes in the spiritual universe; God himself losing the bright attestation of His holiness; Mary Magdalen sitting in heaven beside Herodias; the two thieves entering its gates together, and Judas appearing there long before John. It is incredible that this should be the answer.

The remaining one is the answer of the Gospel, summed up in the text: that God forgives; forgives not capriciously, but with wise, definite, and Divine pre-arrangement; forgives universally, on the ground of an atonement, and on the condition of repentance and faith.—This answer shows God's kindness, holiness, wisdom, together, and fully illustrates what is glorious in Him. It fits precisely to man's sense of need. It makes forgiveness attainable to each, while upholding perfectly the supreme moral order.

And from it we learn the preciousness of the Bible, and gain an argument for its Divine origin; the privilege of accepting God's offer of forgiveness; the infinite hazard, the self-inflicted damage, of neglecting or refusing it.

You will observe, Gentlemen, that I am not proposing this, or either of these, as in any sense a model-plan for one of your sermons. You have an eminent professor to do that, and I could not attempt the office, if I were asked. I only sketch rapidly these possible plans to illustrate, by examples, what I have said: that it is perfectly possible, and very desirable, so to arrange the subject before you that each point when treated shall lead you to the next, and land you in front of it; so that the forward movement of the mind, from first to last, may be wholly unhindered. You require a thorough organization of the subject in your own mind, if you are to present it without a manuscript, with any degree of freedom and vigor. There must be method and progress in your arrangement, or the mind will infallibly be all the while occupied in getting hold of its instruments, not in using them on the people.

It has been said, very admirably, of one brilliant and epigrammatic writer of our day, that "his sentences are like sabre-cuts: they have succession, but not connection." Such a writer, I should think, must read what he writes, or repeat it from memory. There must be connection, as well as succession, in the thoughts which one would express without notes; and the more fully and deeply the plan of the discourse is imbedded in the mind, and made self-suggestive, the more elastic and buoyant is the tread of the mind in all the discussion.

If needful to this result, I would write the plan of the sermon over twenty times, before preaching it; not copying, merely, from one piece of paper upon another, but writing it out, carefully and fully, each time independently, till I perfectly knew it; till it was fixed, absolutely, in the mind. A German, called as a candidate for the jury-box in one of the courts the other day, was asked if he could change, on further evidence, an opinion which he affirmed that he had formed. "No," said he, "I cannot change it, for it is *all mixed up mit my mind!*" The plan of a discourse, if one is to present it without help from a manuscript, should be so absolutely mixed up with his mind that he cannot forget it; that it stays there of itself, and comes up without effort as it is wanted. One may often profitably spend more time, therefore, on the principal arrangement of the subject, and its proper distribution, than on all the collateral and auxiliary details; as they say that more life, if not more labor, was spent on the piles beneath the St. Petersburg church of St. Isaac's, to get a foundation, than on all the magnificent marbles and malachite which have since been lodged in it. It must be a primary, principal aim, in preparing each discourse, to have the ground-work sound and sure, and absolutely established in your mind

It need not be made apparent, perhaps, to the congregation. It is not always best, I think, to have the frame of a sermon like the frame of a Swiss cottage, all shown on the outside. It may be better to keep it within, and to have the presence and the strength of it manifested only in the dignity and stability of the structure which it braces and governs. But it must be there, and give symmetry and security to all the details which grow up upon it.* Saadi, the Persian poet, is quoted by some writer whom I have forgotten, as comparing Fortune to a peacock, "with a showy tail, but a frightful pair of legs." I have sometimes heard sermons which recalled the description. The general arrangement of thoughts in your sermon will constitute the legs, on which it is to move. Be very sure that they are strong, sustaining, progressive; and then let the tail be as God pleases.

When once you have the main plan of the sermon fully in mind, be not too solicitous about

* Note XVII.

minor things, and especially be careful not to let the thoughts become engaged to too many details, which you wish to recall. If you do, you will be as one walking with a thousand minute weights attached to him, each one of them small, but their aggregate amount an overpowering hinderance. It is as good a rule in preaching a sermon as it is in living the Christian life: "lay aside every weight;" every thing, that is, which catches you as with a hook; and the habit of remembering, which so easily winds itself about you; and, being sure of your general governing scheme of thought, let the details, of illustration and expression, be largely those which suggest themselves, either in consequence of previous thought, or without that.

Then if you preach the sermon a second time the hearers will find in it the same general plan, but a different physiognomy. The filling out of the plan will be so different — in forms of statement, subordinate thoughts, illustrative images or examples — that the effect of it will be wholly new. The sermon re-preached will be substan tially as fresh as at first. A clergyman lately deceased, in New England, is reported to have said that 'an old sermon, with a new text, and a new application, is as good as a new one, because of its new collar and cuffs.' But if you follow my different plan, and have the same text, if you like, and the same outline, but with such different subordinate thoughts, whenever you preach, as are then suggested — accepting them as they come, integrating them with the discourse as you proceed — the sermon will be always practically a new one; as related to your mind, as related to your hearers. It will have the same bones, but with a different covering, a different coloring, and in fact a wholly fresh and individual life.

Still further, and FOURTHLY: After this care of your health of body, and your energy of mind, and this careful mastery of the general plan to be followed in the sermon, it is necessary also that you *have command of sufficient subordinate trains of thought to aid you in unfolding and impressing the subject.* — Have images in mind, illustrative instances, whatever may be needed to set forth, exalt, enforce your theme. But never suffer yourselves to be commanded by them. Be always careful to keep yourselves free from any such subjection to them that you will feel bound to recall and reproduce them.

The distinction here is the very obvious and familiar distinction between voluntary recollection, which always implies effort, and involuntary recollection, where things come up to us 'of themselves,' as we say. It is the latter by which we should aid ourselves in preaching, not the former. There are many things which we recall only by a positive exertion; names, dates, the location of unfamiliar towns on the map, the technics of any art, the scientific nomenclature; in general, any thing unconnected and new. Unless my memory deceives me, one of your professors was beginning the study of Hebrew with me in the seminary, when the professor having charge of the class wrote some disconnected characters from the Hebrew alphabet on the black-board, — Aleph, Daleth, Samech, Tsade, and so on, — taking them at hazard, as they occurred to him; and our friend was suddenly asked to pronounce them. After looking a moment he was compelled to confess that, though he knew the old Hebrew gentlemen by sight, to save his life he could not yet call them by name. He got so afterward that he could call them by name, with instant accuracy; and it is wholly unnecessary to praise the progress in that acquaintance which he has since made, or the use he has made of it. But at that early time, to recall them, on the instant, was quite beyond him.

There are other things, however, which one recalls without the slightest conscious effort; which picture themselves upon his mind, with a vividness ineffaceable, and which reäppear when he least is expecting them. The Sistine Madonna, the Transfiguration, some charming Swiss or Italian landscape with lake and mountains, a sunset at sea, the face of a friend — these do not need to be summoned back. They present themselves without our call; and sometimes rise up most distinctly when the thoughts had seemed entirely preöccupied with other things. When the mind is in a fervent and stimulated state, such things occur to it, and a multitude of others, most rapidly and surely. They come in throngs, one suggesting another, all pushing on swiftly for recognition, and if need be for use.

Now it is this involuntary, spontaneous, self-suggesting recollection, by which one who speaks without notes must be aided; and the process of training it to render such assistance is very simple.

In the case of a sermon, for example: as you first think the subject carefully through, subordinate trains of thought will occur, illustrating the main one; passages in literature will be suggested, perhaps; historical examples; Scriptural analogies; scenes in nature, or startling passages in personal experience; all bearing upon the sub ject, and which rise to your mind in instant and fit connection with it.* It is well, I think, to make a brief memorandum of such, indicating them at least by a line or a catch-word on the brief. When you go through the subject again, say on Saturday evening, some of these will again occur, and others will not; but in place of those which do not come back, if your mind is in an active and a fruitful condition, others will suggest themselves. Now look at your notes, and add references to these, noticing again what you previously had thought of, but have now overlooked. Thus you have at a glance before you all that has been suggested to your mind, in connection with the subject. It will be almost certainly more than enough to fill your sermon; and when you finally recall it, in the morning, whatever is best in it will be likely to come back.

Then go and preach; and, in the pulpit, that which had previously approved itself to your mind as fit, striking, germane to the subject,

* Note XVIII.

will again almost certainly be suggested, coming up after its own law, and often in the very words in which it first was presented to the mind. Then give it as it comes. Never stop to recall any thing which you are vaguely and doubtfully conscious of having purposed to say, but which has somehow slipped from your thought. The pause is perilous ; and you probably will not get back what you miss. You have seen a boy, perhaps, pushing his arm between the pickets of a fence to get the round and rolling foot-ball which has fallen beyond it. He can just touch the ball with his fingers, but cannot grasp it ; and the moment he presses it, off it rolls. So it is, often, with the thought which a speaker tries to recover, when he has passed it. It slips away again the instant you reach for it, and will not come back ; while, in the effort to regain it, you have lost your hold upon the congregation.

Men are not responsive to an introverted mind. You never notice, yourselves, what an absent-minded man is saying to you; it is sound, without thought in it. And if your mind is not with the people, but hunting for something back of yourself, you might much better be saying nothing. There is nothing an audience more enjoys than being directly and forcibly addressed, by a full mind, which has studied its subject, and now is pouring out its thought without hesitation, without reserve. But they recoil, and slip from the grasp, the moment they see that your principal effort is to recall things, not to impress things already in mind. They love to be commanded; but they hate the cowardice which springs from a memory imperfect and uneasy.

So avoid this peril. Have plenty of thoughts beforehand in your mind, but let them come to your lips as they will; and if they don't come, never go back for them. They will come again, at some other time; and meantime others which very likely are better, will come in their place, if you go forward. Lord Brougham said of Burke that his finest images are not those which he had meditated beforehand, but those which were struck from his intense mind in the heat of debate: 'like sparks from a working engine, and not like fire-works for mere display.' One can never repeat such passages afterward, with the vividness and force which belonged to them at first. The inspiration of the occasion, which shot its force through them, cannot be replaced.

Dr. Kirk, in the earlier years of that part of his ministry which followed his return from Europe, was wont to preach without full notes, though I think he always used some in the pulpit. Once, when he was preaching at Pittsfield, a gentleman who was sitting in the gallery has told me that he described, toward the end of his sermon, the way of worldly pleasure and gain, without thought of God, as a smooth broad road, along whose easy and gradual slopes men carelessly walked, till they came on a sudden to the precipice at the end; and so vivid was the final image, as it flashed from his mind upon the assembly, that when he depicted them going over the edge, a rough-looking man, who sat next to my friend, rose in his place, and looked over the gallery-front, to see the chasm into which they were falling! The whole figure had doubtless come with a rush to the mind of the preacher. It was as vivid to Dr. Kirk, on the instant of its utterance, as it was to this hearer. The whole swing of the sermon was behind it, as it leaped into speech; and it could not have been repeated, with any thing of the same effect. An effort to reproduce it, afterward, would have been like cutting the flower from stalk and root, to brighten other days with its beauty. What at first was spontaneous, would have then been a matter of mere art and mechanics.

So never go back to remember things, which do not spontaneously come up to your mind while you are speaking. Make as full preparation as you can, but leave it if it lingers. Let the push of your soul be in all that you say, and every sentence be charged with the vitality of an advancing and out-giving mind.

Next week I shall speak of some of the moral and spiritual conditions of success in preaching without one's notes. What I have to say to-day closes here. If you have within you the inspiring conviction that the Gospel has come from the mind of God, and is indispensable to the welfare of man; if you are then careful to keep your whole physical vigor at the highest attainable point, and to keep your mind in a state of corresponding activity and energy; if you make the plan of your sermon simple and natural, and imbed it in your thoughts, so that the mind in treating the subject naturally runs along on that plan, without effort or care, and is all the while free, ready for whatever suggestions may come; if you have sufficient command of subordinate trains of thought, of illustrations, images, historical instances, germane to the subject, but are not yourself commanded by them, and are ready to take them or to leave them according as at the moment they recur, or fail to appear; — then you have, I think, the essential physical and mental conditions of that success which is possible for you. You may speak then with freedom, force, pleasure, and with direct and useful effect on the minds you address; with more effect, I suspect, oftentimes, than if you read a careful essay.

So fulfil these conditions, Gentlemen: and then follow the advice which Jehoshaphat gave, when he set of the priests and the chief of the fathers to be judges in Israel, and gave them their motto, — among the grandest, I think, in all history; certainly there is none like it in the Kaiser-saal at Frankfurt, under all the portraits of German emperors which there are assembled, — "Deal courageously; and the Lord shall be with the good!"

THIRD LECTURE.

Mr. President: Young Gentlemen: —

IN each of these talks to you I illustrate in myself, as I am quite aware, one of the disadvantages connected with the practice of speaking without notes; a disadvantage which becomes especially noticeable, and especially important, when one has a large subject to present, the treatment of which must be compressed into a comparatively small space of time.

I have been conscious every time, after speaking to you, that there were many things which I had not touched, of which I should have been glad to speak if the hour had permitted, and if I had not spoken under the pressure of its sharp limitations. I feel the same thing more keenly to-day, because each of the points which I have to present is deserving of special and separate treatment, and might reasonably occupy a full hour by itself: while I have to present them all within the same limits, or as near that as I can. It seems like trying to squeeze the thousand volumes of a library into one book-case: or to pack the entire furniture of a room in a couple of trunks.

I shall be constrained to treat the subjects rapidly, cursorily, in a way which I fear will seem to your minds, as well as to my own, unsatisfactory. But I have no alternative, having no other afternoons on which I could properly ask you to hear me, or, indeed, on which I could promise to meet you here. I must therefore do briefly, in a summary way, what it would be pleasanter to do more at leisure, with larger scope; since whatever I am to say must be finished to-day.

In the last talk I spoke, as you will remember, of certain physical and mental conditions of success in preaching without one's manuscript. These are, all of them, important in themselves. But they become still more important as connected with others, moral and spiritual, which are to them ulterior and supreme. First comes always, in God's arrangement, that which is natural; and, afterward, that which is spiritual. The conditions which I have to-day to present stand in this Divine order; and they come last because they are highest. They are not, indeed, important only to one who speaks without his notes. They are important also, perhaps as much so, to one who carefully writes his sermons. But they are indispensable to the first; and it is his need, his proper self-discipline and equipment of mind, which I am trying to set before you. I should leave the whole subject, therefore, most inadequately treated, if I did not proceed to speak of these, as I intend to do to-day.

The FIRST of them which I specify is this: One should have *a distinct and an energetic sense of the importance of that particular subject on which he is to preach at the time.*

I said, at the beginning of the lecture last week, that the minister should have, as a necessary pre-requisite to any real success whatever, a serious, paramount, inspiring sense of the Divine origin and authority of the Gospel, and of its transcendent importance to men. This is indispensable to success in preaching, either with notes or without them. Unless one has it, it is hard to see why he should enter the ministry it all; and if he does, he will be almost certain to fail, — not understanding his own errand in the world, and not having his forces fully drawn forth by the truth which he presents.

I do not now repeat, you observe, what I then said; but I add to it this essential particular, that he should have also a distinct, animating, inspiring impression of the importance of that individual subject upon which he is at the time to preach — of the theme which he has immediately in hand.

It has such importance, if it is really a part of the Gospel; and if it is not, he ought not to bring it to the pulpit at all. As compared with other truths embraced in the great complex harmony of Revelation, it may not have a superior, possibly not even an equal, importance. There are orders and hierarchies in the Divine realms, both of being and of truth. Not every doctrine is so fundamental as is that of human depravity. Not every fact is so central in the Gospel as is that of the Passion and the Cross. Not every truth is so dominant and supreme as is that of the Judgment to come. It is not every particular in the life of the Lord which has such importance in itself, or such a power to quicken us, as has the Resurrection. It is not every one of the Psalms which is so attractive or so impressive to the Christian heart as is the twenty-third or the fifty-first.

At the same time it is true that, as compared with the subjects which ordinarily engage the attention of men, any theme suggested by the

Gospel to the mind of the preacher — which is itself a part of that Gospel — has an intrinsic, a continuing, a surpassing importance. It is a part of the whole structure, as is every part of the stately column, — base, shaft, capital, and the very volutes upon it. It is important to all the rest, as is every member of the human frame, — the eye, the ear, the finger, and the foot, as well as the nobler heart and brain. It is a part of the Divine word; one of God's thoughts, which He has spoken to the world, through men inspired of the Holy Ghost. And if it was worth while for Him to speak it, certainly it is worth while for us each one to meditate upon it, and proclaim it to others.

It has, too, its own great office to accomplish. It is one of the instruments which God means to use for quickening and renewing the souls of men; which is in fact used, by the Spirit of God, for that august end. Whether, therefore, it seem to us more or less important in itself, if employed for that sublime result it has immense and immortal value and you can never say before hand whether this or that particular truth shall be the means which God will use. Sometimes He takes the humblest truth, as it looks to us, and makes it most efficient to accomplish His end. The rod of Moses had no power in itself to roll back the waves, or to make them again return in strength; but God gave it such power. The mantle of Elijah had no charm in itself to divide the waters of Jordan when it smote them; but God gave it its efficiency. And sometimes, as if to magnify his grace, and set forth most fully the glory and the choice of His sovereign will, He makes what seems to man unimportant the instrument of His greatest work. A narrative may do more than a large and careful development of doctrine. A portrait of character, or of any trait in it, may bless men more than precept, or argument, or an elaborate exposition of prophecy. What seems the least becomes often the mightiest, when the push of God's Spirit is behind it.

Always, therefore, remember that the special truth which you are to treat has importance in itself, and may be the instrument in the Hand above for accomplishing the work toward which your entire labor is tending; and then engage your mind to it for the time, as if no other subject existed. Keep it in distinct and quickening contemplation. Be the 'man of one idea,' till your sermon is ended; and let that idea be the one before you.

It is not difficult to do this. All that you need is to hold the subject before your thoughts until its relation to God's mind, on the one hand, and to His revelation, and on the other to the minds of your hearers, is evident to you, and you have felt the impression of it. It is one of the best tests of a subject, of its intrinsic solidity and value, if it will bear such intent and continuing meditation. If it will, it will bear discussion in the pulpit. You may throw your whole weight on it, without diffidence or reserve. But if it shrinks, as you consider it, gives way, shows weakness, depend upon it it is some theory of your own, which has not the validity that belongs to God's truth. Take the iron-pyrites. It sparkles like gold, and you think for the moment that it is gold, perhaps. But when you lift it in your hand, it is light. When you touch it with the fire of chemical analysis, you detect the fumes of sulphur in it; while the gold, with no more gleam on its surface, is solid and pure. In like manner, take a subject, look at it on all sides, hold it before your attentive scrutiny, till you have ascertained all that is in it; and then, if it still satisfies your mind, and quickens your heart, it is a subject to preach upon.

Nor is it at all dangerous to do this. It is sometimes objected that a preacher will become one-sided and narrow, will preach only on a given set of subjects, if he follows this method, of absorbing himself for the time altogether in the theme which is before him. But there is not half so much danger of this in preaching without a manuscript as with one. I have known one man who preached so long on the doctrine of Sin that there seemed no room remaining in his mind for the promise of Salvation ; and another who preached upon Fore-ordination, till one was really tempted to apply to him the rough remark of Robert Hall about a minister who did the same thing in the neighborhood of Bristol — that 'he must have been fore-ordained, from all eternity, to be a fool.' And I have known one who preached upon Baptism, himself a pædo-baptist, till the people were not only showered but soaked with it. Each one of these men wrote his sermons !

You will remember, perhaps, what I said in my first talk, a fortnight ago, about the necessity of discharging the mind of each subject, successively, when it has been treated ; of putting it thoroughly out of your thoughts, and taking another in its place. This is difficult, certainly ; especially at first. But it can be accomplished ; and one can form the habit of doing it, till it shall be easy, and a matter of course. Do this, then, regularly. When you have preached on one subject divest your mind of it, and take another. In that way treat each subject, as it occurs, amply, cordially, eagerly, with enthusiasm, with the whole force of your mind and your will centred upon it for the time ; and as, by degrees, you go the round of that great system which lies before you in the Scripture, ultimately you will have treated, with fulness and force, the whole circle of Christian truth, precept, and promise.

If your subject, for example, is the nature of faith, keep it specific. Do not allow it to become mixed in your thought with any thing else. Conceive in your own mind, and show to others, precisely what it is — this penitent and loving confidence in God, who is declared to us in Christ ; which has in it the element of power and holiness, and which is the condition of life eternal. Have it as clear before yourselves, make it as clear before your hearers, as was the outline of Grace Church tower and spire to me a few minutes since, as I walked up Broadway.

Or, if your subject is the power of faith, treat that as distinctly; until the essential heroism of spirit of which it is the parent comes vividly before you and your people; till they see that faith is everywhere the real heroic and conquering force — that which drives the explorer through thick-ribbed ice of Arctic seas; that which sends the traveller through tangled forests, malarious swamps, and stony deserts of Central Africa; that which pushed Columbus across the sea to find this continent, in spite of the constant fears of his sailors that if he went further his ship would slide over the rim of the planet.

Faith is the true power of heroism, over the world; not in religion only, but in all common and secular affairs. It gives the power that moves mankind. Dwell upon that, then, in your thoughts, and make it plain and palpable to others, till they with you cannot help but see the connection there is, and the reason of the connection, between evangelical faith on earth and the vision on high — the hope to which it here inspires, the heaven which there it swiftly opens.

So if your subject be one of those specific graces which Peter commands to be added to faith — courage, knowledge, self-restraint, patient endurance — either of those which he would have led up by the Christian, hand in hand, as in the Greek chorus: consider it with discriminating attention; treat it distinctively; show its relation to the entrance which shall by-and-by be richly ministered, as by a chorus of saints and angels, into the kingdom of God's glory. If it be a doctrine, of human depravity: feel it yourselves, and make others feel it; the depth, the energy, the consequences of it. So, equally, if it be regeneration, atonement; or if it be only a prophecy that you interpret, a biography that you sketch, a passage in history on which you throw light, a parable whose meaning you interpret. Whatever your subject be, let it be for the time the one engrossing subject of your mind; and until you have preached on it let nothing come in to divert in the least attention from it.

Carlyle says somewhere, in his half-cynical fashion, that "the candid judge will in general require that a speaker, in so extremely serious a universe as this of ours, have something to speak about."* It is a good rule. Your congregation will hold you to it; and the only way to meet their just and constant demand upon you is by having the mind thus centred upon a subject, filled with its meaning, made alive with its influence.

Here is one vital advantage in preaching without one's notes before him. I said in my first talk that there was a certain disadvantage in this, in the matter of exchanges; because these do not give the relief, when the manuscript is wanting, which they otherwise would. But there is a greater disadvantage, so far as the congregation is concerned, in using the essay. No enthusiasm may go with it, or out from it upon others. A

* Miscellanies, vol. iv. p. 311; review of Scott's Life

sermon which is read, without having been re-absorbed in the mind, never has vital virtue in it. I have heard such read in my own pulpit — manuscript sermons, yellow with time; and, while I would not undertake to set bounds to God's omnipotence, I have said to myself as the reading went on, 'there is not the least natural tendency in a thousand such sermons to convert a mouse.' But if you follow the course I have outlined, and throw your whole enthusiasm for the time into the subject which you are treating, when you are abroad as when you are at home, there will no doubt be labor in it, but the labor will bring its great reward, in the glory of God, and the good of those whom you address.

Three years ago, on a beautiful Easter Sunday, I went into an Anglican Chapel in France, and heard a sermon, of fifteen or eighteen minutes' length, on the Lord's Resurrection. At the close, the preacher said: "And now if there be any among you who to-day have come hither simply upon the cold legs of custom, then" —

so and so. I thought it not an impressive address, considering the brightness and warmth of the day, and that many of us were there for the first time in our life. But I say to you, Young Gentlemen: If any of you ever go into the pulpit 'simply upon the cold legs of custom,' be very careful to take a manuscript with you. But if you go to speak to the assembly because your mind is full of the truth, and you long to impart that truth to them, for their sakes and for God's sake, — then charge your mind with it, and speak it with all the force you can give it, without any notes.

And SECONDLY: To speak freely and usefully without notes one should have, from the very beginning of his discourse, distinctly in view, *a definite end, of practical impression, which his discourse is to make and leave on the minds before him.* — He must speak for a purpose; and the purpose must propel and govern the sermon.

Of course this is not peculiar to unwritten sermons. Every sermon should have such an end, of practical impression, present from the outset to him who prepares it, both while he is preparing and when he is preaching it. But this is absolutely indispensable to one who is to preach without aid from notes. Otherwise the force of his moral nature will never be enlisted in the work he has in hand.

Your venerable Presbyterian Form of Government says — or the Introduction to it says — that "Truth is in order to goodness." I do not live under that Form of Government precisely, and so perhaps I should prefer to modify somewhat that form of expression. Truth, I take it, is in its essence the reality of things; and truth, in expression, is the representation of that reality. It does not exist, therefore, I suppose, with reference to any thing ulterior to itself. It is, 'whether or no;' without regard to consequences. But certainly Truth is declared to us, the Divine Truth, in order to its specific impression upon life and character; and that, I take it, is really the import of this statement.

The whole Bible bears on practical results; and here is one great secret of its power. In this, as in other things, it is unique and supreme in the world's literature. It is not a mere collection of interesting biographies, historical narratives, precepts, arguments, proverbs, songs; but it all bears, from first to last, on definite results, — the conversion of men to God, their upbuilding in righteousness. Whoever preaches, then, on themes derived by him from the Bible, should have the same end distinctly in view.*

It is necessary, as I said, in order to enlist his moral nature, ardently, thoroughly, in the work he has to do. Intellectual excitement is relatively without warmth. Intellectual enthusiasm, for a proposition which has no special practical relation to those to whom it is being presented, never has the force of real passion in it. The heating power in the nature of man is in its moral element. This gives the inward glow and vividness to all his intellectual processes, when it

* Note XIX.

inspires them. Power and impulse always come from it.

The desire after practical usefulness is, therefore, indispensable to one who would preach well without his notes. He may be logical, in the absence of it; but his will never be "logic on fire," till his moral nature has clearly in view an end toward which it is steadily working, pushing the instrumental intellectual force, till that also glows with it.

The minister requires this, also, as an intellectual corrective and stimulant; to give unity to his discourse, progressiveness, steadiness, and an easy celerity, to his mental operations. Without it, he will be like the ship tossing on the waves, hither and yon, in the darkness of a fog. The fog lifts; the headland, or the light, appears; and instantly the ship swings into her course. Instead of heaving idly about, passive on the rolling waters, making every one sea-sick, she steadies on an even keel, catches the wind upon her wings, and flies toward the point the posi tion of which has now been revealed. So an ultimate foreseen *point d'appui*, a rallying point for all parallel or converging lines of the discourse, is necessary to give steady and swift progressiveness to the mind which moulds and delivers that discourse. The converging of all subordinate thoughts into one grand thought, to be pressed upon the hearer, then is secured; like the convergence of the streams running toward a 'clove' in the line of the hills. Hither and thither, northward, southward, run the brooks, yet ever meeting and mingling into one, as they draw toward the gap, till the thousand trickles become a torrent as they pour at last through the gate into the valley. So all collateral thoughts, arguments, illustrations of a sermon, when bearing upon a single end of moral impression, combine their forces, rush together at last in a common channel, and strike with heavy impact on the mind.

This is necessary, too, to keep men from yielding to that habit of discursiveness which is the easily besetting sin of many full minds, and which is absolutely fatal to one who is speaking without his notes. No matter how brilliant the mind may be, how richly stocked with historical knowledges, how prolific in fancy, image, felicitous phrase, — this habit of discursiveness will weary out the most patient congregation.

You hear one begin, for example, with some saying of the Master to John the Baptist, or to one of his disciples. First he describes the scenery, of the Jordan valley, or of the shores around the sea of Tiberias; then the persons, to whom the saying was addressed; then the possible relations of John the Baptist to the sect of the Essenes; then the relations of this sect to the others, and to the whole Herodian family; then he plunges into the interminable tangle of the Herodian genealogy, and shows the relations of this one and that one to the Roman emperors; then of the Roman empire itself to the ancient civilization, with a tracing out of the roots and the fruits of that civilization; and then he goes kiting, at large, through the universe; — till the hour is ended before he has fairly got back to his text! Nobody can stand such preaching a great while. The most patient listener will wish by-and-by that the man's brain would explode, and so make an end.* The best corrective to such a dangerous tendency of mind is to have an end, of practical impression, always in view, from the outset on. As soon as you give one a purpose to be accomplished, things will fall into their places; extraneous things will be instinctively, and of course, ruled out; there will be motion and current to his speech.

This is important, also, as it regards the mere matter of style. Studious men, dwelling in 'the solitary and still air of delightful studies,' are apt to get a style which reminds one of the remark that some one has made of the style of Tertullian — "splendid, but dark, like polished ebony." Or, it is stiff, with interwoven threads of gold, — like a rich brocade, beautiful to look

* Note XX.

upon, beautiful for parade, but not fitting the limbs, not furnishing a habit in which the mind may freely walk and freely work. That is the tendency with studious men; whose literary enthusiasm is apt to get the mastery over their practical evangelical zeal. Their style is sure to become too stately.

On the other hand, there is a dangerous tendency in speaking without notes to a mere wash of words, a debilitating fluency, in which is neither head nor point; where nothing arrests and strikes attention, rouses the imagination, awakens historical recollection, elevates or animates any power where all is a dreary out-pour of verbiage, incessantly coming, like the ribbons in a juggler's trick. "What color will you have, Gentlemen?" and out it comes; twenty yards of blue, and then twenty of pink, and more and more as it is ordered. The man who thus speaks seems to be pulling or pumping words out of some bottomless reservoir within, without the smallest possible reference to any result to be accomplished; and his own feeling, his own thought-power, washes away on the flux of his words. No single quality which style ought to have is present, or is possible, under such conditions.

Dr. Emmons used to say that 'style should be like window-glass, perfectly transparent, and with very little sash.'* That is good, so far as it goes; but there are certain important qualities of style which are not covered by that description. I should say, rather, that style is to thought what the body is to the spirit. It should be itself vital, with a life of its own, sympathetic and responsive to the thought within. It should be proportionate, symmetrical, with whatever of beauty may properly belong to it. It should be gentle enough to fondle a child, facile enough to laugh or sing, strong enough to strike a heavy blow, for righteousness or in self-defence, when occasion calls for it. That is always the best style which answers most perfectly to the

* Note XXI.

thought within, as the body to the spirit. And you can get such a style as that, fashion it, keep it, only by work. You do not get it in the Seminary, nor out of books. You get it by preaching, with a practical aim distinctly in view; by letting your thought wreak itself upon expression, while it is urgent and hot within you. Thus you gain the expression most natural to yourself, in your best moods; and always you will find that that mode of expression which to you is most natural is also to others most effective and powerful.

Observe the plain uneducated man: how well he talks, when he has an end to accomplish by it! The silent man, silent in all common assemblies, — there comes a time when something calls out the force within him, some story to be told, some enterprise to be urged, some friend to be championed; and he speaks with freedom, promptness, power. Without knowing it himself he almost realizes Milton's description of a true eloquence: 'his words, like so many nimble and airy servitors, trip about him at command, and in well-ordered files, as he would wish, fall aptly into their own places.' *

Hear the lawyer, on some important occasion, when life is imperilled, or personal liberty, or when large properties or great reputations are suddenly at stake. You have heard him as a lecturer, perhaps, and thought him dull, or merely rhetorical — more intent on pleasing himself with his fancies and phrases than on pushing his thought into your mind. But now, before the jury, when these great interests are depending upon him, how full of force, impulse, persuasive enthusiasm, are his words! His style itself is radically transformed. Every sentence is sharpened, compacted, inspired, by his endeavor to gain his end. The intensity of his purpose puts vigor and swiftness into his speech. The supreme energy, the real δεινότης in utterance, only then comes forth.

Still further, too, it must be remembered that

* Note XXII.

a man who is intently at work to accomplish practical results by his preaching will pray over his sermons, a great deal more than will another not so moved; and so he will get the inspiring help, the unction, and the grace, which come from communion with the Divine Mind. The closet will help the pulpit; and there is no force or brilliance of mind, no fulness of knowledge, which can make the sermon what it may be and should be, without this touch from above upon it.

So always have in view, Gentlemen, a definite end to be accomplished in preaching. Remember Paul's maxim: "I press toward the mark." It is as good and true in sermonizing, as it is in Christian life and character. Have an aim in the sermon; and never be satisfied till the sermon is as fit as you can make it to accomplish that aim. A man in the Seminary with me once said, "I like to discuss subjects; but I never know what to do with them, after they are discussed. I can only leave them, and go along." Such a man should always write his sermons, if he preaches at all; as an army should shelter itself in a fortress, when it cannot or dare not meet its enemy in the field; as a man-of-war should blaze away at a distance, when it has no pikes or cutlasses to board with. But if you are intent upon practical ends, to which your whole force shall contribute, then the manuscript may go. For then your mind will gain force, foresight, energy, from its purpose; and will give whatever of power and beauty are natural to it to the very style of expression through which you seek to lead men to the throne of God.*

THIRDLY: *Have in view individual hearers in the congregation,* on whom you desire to make your impression, and with whose needs you are familiar; to whom, therefore, your sermon is particularly adapted, both while you study and when you preach it.

I am inclined to think that here was an advantage, — perhaps I should modify that

* Note XXIII.

remark, and say that here was the advantage if anywhere, — in the old way of preparing men for the ministry, under the care of a particular pastor, as compared with the way in which you are being trained, and in which I was trained, in a Seminary; under more learned, scientific, and laborious teachers. I think those men learned to be interested in persons, where we learn chiefly to be interested in subjects. They came in contact with individual minds, in a way which helped them in all their ministry, though their training was certainly less elaborate, systematic, and scholastic, than ours.

Perhaps this disadvantage in the modern system is compensated, doubtless it is diminished, by the facilities which now abound for work in mission-schools, Bible-classes, prayer-meetings. I know, in my own experience, that I learned some things from a Bible-class, which I taught in the village-church at Andover, which have been as valuable to me in subsequent life as any thing which I learned from the magnificent lectures which during the week I attended and enjoyed. I presume it is equally true of you. If not in this way, then in some other, you must get into vital contact with persons, as well as with themes. Otherwise your real force will never come out. The rays of light get heating power by being focussed through a lens, and made to converge upon one point. So a man's mental action becomes intense, penetrating, effective, as it contemplates a definite effect, on personal minds.

Here was one great secret, certainly, of Dr. Nettleton's power. I do not know that his sermons would seem extraordinary to us, if we should now read them; since we are not the persons whom he had in view in preparing and preaching them. But they were immensely effective at the time, because he had before him individuals, with whose states of mind he was familiar, and to whom the truth as presented by him was exquisitely adjusted, with every effort and every art. As a "fisher of men" he surpassed every one in the skill and assiduity with which he angled for particular souls. Thousands of anecdotes illustrate this. Accordingly he worked with immense facility, sometimes preparing or remodelling sermons every day for weeks together, and preaching them afterward, with an interest in them which saved him from exhaustion; because his thought was intently fixed on the persons whom by means of them he would reach.

So it is with the lawyer. See him before the jury, in a case where his convictions are strong, and his feelings are enlisted. He saw long ago, as he glanced over the box, that five of those in it were sympathetic with him; as he went on, he became equally certain of seven; the number now has risen to ten; but two are still left, whom he feels that he has not persuaded or mastered. Upon them he now concentrates his power, summing up the facts, setting forth anew and more forcibly the principles, urging upon them his view of the case, with a more and more intense action of his mind upon theirs, until one only is left. Like the blow of a hammer, continually repeated, till the iron bar crumbles beneath it, his whole force comes, with ceaseless percussion, on that one mind, till it has yielded, and accepts the conviction on which the pleader's purpose is fixed. Men say, afterward, "he surpassed himself." It was only because the singleness of his aim gave unity, intensity, an overpowering energy, to the mind it incited.

I remember perfectly that the first time I ever had any thorough sense of freedom, facility, self-forgetfulness in preaching, was when, some twenty-five years ago, a gentleman of my parish — an unusually able and cultivated man, who had occupied high political and social positions, and for whom I had great respect — told me that he was practically a fatalist. He did not use the word, but that was what his language meant. He believed that every thing came to pass as God intended and wished that it should, and that all things would come out right in the end

There he would leave the whole matter, of life and of the future. Well: that struck at the foundation of human responsibility. It ruled the Bible out of the world, both law and salvation, at one sweep. It in fact invalidated human law; taking from it all moral elements of authority and sacredness, and converting it into a simple mandate of force, for the conservation of material interests. I was determined, if possible, to push that notion out of his mind: and I remember now the enjoyment which I had, and the easy vigor with which I wrought, in taking up an argument, weighing it, seeing precisely how it bore upon this point; then treating another in like manner, and another; combining them, bringing them in from different and unexpected points, — until it seemed to me the demonstration was absolute, certainly to my mind, hopefully to his. When I came to preach with that concentrated aim, that intense desire and continuing purpose to reach if possible the one mind for which the whole sermon had been arranged, preaching was as easy as flight to the bird, or swimming to the fish. It was simply the natural motion of the mind, charged with its subject, filled with the argument, and intent upon the end which the argument was to serve.

Before that my sermons had been always, I think, like the general cannonading which precedes the real shock of battle. A hundred guns thundering away against the Cemetery-hill at Gettysburg, and a hundred guns in tremendous reply: all uproar and smoke, but nobody hurt! It is the rifle-ball that does the business. So never confine yourselves to the contemplation of themes. Make themes your means for reaching persons; and give the mind force, by giving it concentration.

The true evangelical fervor comes in this way, with affectionate interest in personal souls. The Lord himself did not come to the world to publish elaborate discourses to men. He was full of the truth; and the truth flashed from him, as the occasion suggested. A sneering objection brought one discourse from him ; an affectionate inquiry elicited another; the dullness of his disciples incited another. And all the radiance which fills the gospels, flowing from His mind over the world, was first drawn forth by the minds around Him, to which He would minister light, comfort, purity, hope. In this, as in all else, the disciple should strive to be like his Lord.

Observe, too, what variety you secure in this way, in the subjects which you treat: how perfectly you avoid the danger, which may otherwise be a great one, of having a limited series of subjects, on which your mind most easily works, and to which it returns with readiest facility. You avoid this wholly, if your preaching has persons always in view, and not merely subjects. For there are all sorts of minds in a congregation, and in all sorts of states. Here is a sceptic, perhaps propagating his scepticism, who is to be answered, silenced, if possible convinced. Here is a person not sceptical in temper, but teased with unwelcome and disturbing doubts, which you are to try to remove and disperse. Here is one indifferent, whom you must arouse, and startle into attention to the truth; another, inquiring, undecided, whom you must urge into the way of righteousness. There are sinners to be converted, and sufferers to be soothed; the tempted, who are to be warned and taught; the imperfectly developed in Christian grace, who need education in particular qualities; the poor who must be cheered, the rich who must be taught a more generous liberality, — that "it *is* more blessed to give than to receive."

Your congregation is always a microcosm. Little children are in it, as well as adults; the aged, as well as the young and strong; all classes of minds, in all sorts of relations, each with a different Past behind it. If you preach then to individuals, you will find subjects multiplying on your hands. Faster than you can use them, they will come. As you take each class, or case, in turn, you will be really going the round of the Christian scheme, and unconsciously will be giving it a development as cosmic and many-sided as itself.

And when you thus preach to individuals, be sure that you do not give over till you have, if possible, secured success. Don't think because you have preached the work is done; or because an impression is strong on your mind, that it must of necessity be equally strong upon the minds to which you would transfer it. A minister is always tempted to feel that because his argument is convincing to himself, it must be to others; that because he has personally reached a high point, of feeling and vision, he has carried up everybody with him to the same It may not be so at all. Your expectation may be very far from being realized; your preaching be less effective than you suppose, and the response to it very different. Remember that you preach amidst influences which work all the while against your efforts, and which, not unfrequently, push out the truth faster and further than you can insert it; so that the same man who on Sunday was moved as if by a word from God himself, has forgotten it all before Monday is ended. One who weeps to-day may scoff to-morrow, and the feeling of the sanctuary may disappear altogether in Broadway or Wall Street. So keep up your acquaintance with the minds you address, and never expect too much from any one sermon.

A lady coming home on one of the steamships that cross the Atlantic, on the first day out saw a half-drunken sailor, who was insolent to the mate, knocked down on the spot, with a heavy blow. The blood gushed from his nostrils; his face puffed up in swollen and purple ridges, beneath the stroke:—it was to her simply frightful! She was sickened by it, and left the deck. Below, she soon became sea-sick; and three or four days passed before she again could come upon deck. Then she saw the same man standing at the wheel; and going swiftly up to him, she asked, with womanly sympathy: "How's your head to-day?" "West, nor'west, and running free," was the answer that staggered her. He had wholly forgotten what to her had given that startling shock. You laugh at this; but you will often find that it just about parallels the depth and the permanence of the impression which you make by the sermons on which you most rely. What you thought sure to be fruitful, and to abide, has gone from the memory of those whom you especially addressed, before the morrow's sun is up. So never give up your thought of individuals, and your purpose to reach them with the truth, until you know that success is attained.

And FOURTHLY: *Always carry with you into the pulpit a sense of the immense consequences which may depend on your full and faithful presentation of the truth.*

There will be such consequences depending on it; since, when you preach, you are bringing the grandest moral force which the world has known into contact with minds constitutionally adapted to receive and retain impressions from it. It is not from ancient history, or law, that you are to draw your lessons and your motives. It is not from ethics, or speculative philosophy. It is from the world supernatural, the realms invisible; from beings, and facts, Divine and eternal. Hence come the influences which you are set to make influential upon men's minds; from the Advent, and the Ascension; from Sinai, and from Calvary; from the manger at Bethlehem, and the Judgment throne. If you feel the impression of these on yourselves, and so preach to others — if you are each a living Gospel, believing the word, and preaching it because you are moved thereto by its own force — you have a tremendous instrument to use. Then your spirit will help your words. You will become true priests for God, radiating to others the influence which first has come to yourselves from Divine revelation.

And you use this instrument, accomplish this

office, in circumstances the most helpful: in the shelter of the sanctuary; in the assembly of communing souls; with auxiliary services, appropriate for the further impression of the truth; on the Lord's Day,—that still harbor in the week, surrounded by the breakwater of even human law, on whose tranquil bosom the soul is sheltered from the tumults of time. You are to bring the Gospel, then and there, into contact with the minds before you. There must be an impression from it, falling with power on those who hear it. This cannot be otherwise. It may work in one direction, it may work in another. It is like the sunshine, which touches the meadows, and makes them bloom in brighter verdure, which touches the sand, and makes it more dry and vitreous than it was: which touches one metallic plate, treated with iodine, and turns it purple; another, treated with nitrate of silver, and turns it black. Some will resist your influence: you cannot help it. Some will accept, and be forever quickened by it; and this shall be to you a joy. You will feel, then, that you are accomplishing the noblest office which God ever gives to man on earth; since the issue of your work is an influence upon character, and an influence upon character involves influence upon destiny — immortal destinies flowing from character.*

In revivals men feel this; and it makes the dull eloquent as they feel it. At all times we should feel it, when we enter the pulpit to declare to men God's message of grace. Oftentimes, when we are wholly unaware, there are minds in the congregation approaching the fateful point of transition from one course to another, like men riding side by side in a railway carriage till they reach the point where their paths diverge. They have come from Montreal to Rutland, perhaps; riding together all the way. There, one of them steps to another seat. For a space their tracks run parallel still, but by degrees they diverge; further, and further,

* Note XXIV.

they go asunder; till, of the two so lately riding and talking together, one has reached Boston, Liverpool, Berlin, the other San Francisco, Yokohama, Hong Kong. Side by side, a few weeks since, and now the diameter of the earth between them! At any time there may be before you minds approaching such critical points in their experience; the turning-points, from which the whole course of their life shall run, in one direction or the other, forevermore. No circle of the centuries shall again bring them together. You do not know when these moments come; and should always preach as if, among those whom you address, there might be some who had reached them now.

What a striking thing that is in the crowded and radiant gospel of John, full of sublimest discourses and events, when he says in speaking of his first meeting with the Master: "It was about the tenth hour"! About the tenth hour? Why put so unimportant a circumstance into a gospel so brief at the best, and where sublime things have hardly room? There is nothing strange in it. John could not forget, and must insert it. It was the first time he had talked with Him whose love and wisdom became there after his inspiration, in life, and death, and the hereafter; and the very moment was vivid still before his recollection. He remembered just how high the sun was, above the western Mediterranean, at that supreme point in his experience. He remembers it now. So there are moments in the experience of many, when they heard from the pulpit words of power, declaring to them God's love in Christ, which will be memorable to them forever, — as long as the issues of the choices which they made continue tc unfold.

You will not discern the presence of such moments, when you are speaking; but never forget that they may come, in any sermon. And so let the consequences possibly depending on your faithful and full presentation of the truth be always distinctly present to you.*

* Note XXV.

The thought of them will inspire you to the best use of every power which you possess, that you may make the highest thought, the widest study, converge upon present and practical results. It will have the effect to dignify and ennoble the mind itself; stirring it up, as the statesman is stirred, on the great occasion, as the lawyer, when pleading for life in peril; making it robust, manly, eager. It will make one serious, too, reverent, modest; and will keep him, absolutely, from resorting to those tricks, antics, grimaces, which seem now-a-days to be coming into fashion, and which are perhaps more likely to be adopted by those who preach without their notes than by those who carefully write their sermons.

In regard to these eccentricities of manner, I, for one, would speak with caution. I am certainly no precisian, in regard to gesture or speech in the pulpit. I believe that every man should use the power which God has given him, in the way most natural, under the impulse of the supreme consciousness that God is speaking His truth through him. If the teachings of any professor hindered me from that, with all respect and affection for him I would forget his instructions as soon as I could. If Dr. Blair's volumes stood in the way of it, I would tie those volumes in one big package, and make a nice grave for them, in the garden or the sea. Let men speak with the purpose of reaching, helping, blessing others ; and each according to his own idiom, of nature and of habit.*

But there is oftentimes a tendency, not to be individual, idiomatic, in speech, but to be theoretical, imitative. Because one preacher gestures with his heels, — as Mr. Choate was once said to do,— a young man thinks that he must do the same. Because one drops his voice to a whisper, and follows with tremendous explosions of sound, somebody else feels bound to do likewise. He becomes in fact, without intending it, a hypocrite, in the original sense — ὑποκριτής, an actor

* Note XXVI.

Then he finds, very likely, that something *outré* and sensational in style draws an assembly, and so he seeks to reproduce that; till he comes to be full, in his own utterance, of a second-hand sensational bosh, without substance or sense, — reminding one of what an English lady said of the shop-windows in Paris, during the Prussian siege: that "they showed fifty pots of mustard to an ounce of meat."

Eccentricity is undoubtedly sometimes legitimate; the privilege of an anomalous mind. Surprising and startling things sometimes are useful; irritants of an attention which would otherwise fail. But when one attempts to imitate these, to ape eccentricity, to systematize surprises, and to put on the manner of somebody else, he is simply contemptible, and certain to fail. Yet when the itch for this thing, and for the transient notoriety which it brings, has once got into a man, there is no friction that I know of, of critical ointments, that will take it out. Nothing but a thorough alterative will do it;

and the only proper alterative is, a sense of the far-extending consequences which depend on his ministry. That will make him serious, sober; too grave for grimaces, and too thoughtful for tricks.*

It will keep him, too, from yielding to the temptations to negligence and indolence. I do not know whether it was Occom, the Mohegan preacher to the Montauk Indians, or some other Indian candidate for the ministry — Dr. Prime perhaps could tell us — who was asked before the Presbytery the question which your Professor of Theology is very likely to ask of some of you: "What is original sin?" and who answered that 'he didn't know what other people's might be, but he rather thought that his was *laziness*.' There are many others who suffer from the same, very radical in the soul; and it often develops into actual transgression. You will be more in danger from it, if you have some facility in extemporaneous speech. You are busy with

* Note XXVII.

other things during the week; you postpone any thorough preparation for the Sunday; you find that for a time your people will be satisfied, at least the unreflecting will be, with something which has not cost much labor; and after a while you come to intermit all careful and thorough analysis of subjects, and to trust to superficial suggestions, and to hasty and careless forms of speech. It will work like dry-rot, eating out the heart of your strength. Water does not run down hill more surely than such a man declines in power.

The way to guard against it is, to bear in mind, as before, the transcendent consequences which connect themselves with what you do, in the pulpit, and before you enter it. Then you will feel that you must not enter it without full preparation; that the interests involved are too sacred and high. Your pulpit will be the throne of your thoughts, through all the week. Nothing else will seriously divert your mind from the work to be done in it.

The same contemplation, of results to be realized through your ministrations, will help to form in you that instinct of skill in your work of preaching which no Seminary can teach; which you must each one gain for yourselves, by practice, experience, self-discipline, observation. There is such a practical instinct of skill, in every art, and every profession; which gives the intuitive law of success, and shows the only way to reach it; by which one can instantly use his powers, to the greatest advantage, with the utmost facility, for accomplishing his ends. You see it everywhere. One man takes aim at the target carefully, and misses it wholly; another simply raises his rifle, apparently without aim, and the obedient bullet strikes the bull's-eye. One man pitches and rolls in the surf-boat, wholly unable to reach the shore, till a wave overturns him, and he is flung upon the sand gasping and drenched; another slides in on the incoming breaker, and before an imperceptible turn of the oar the boat rides smoothly to the beach, landing him high and dry on its safe ridges.

So, everywhere, there is this instinct of skill; which the preacher needs to get, like all other workmen; which he can get only by earnest, continuous, conscientious work, in view of the results which depend on his work. When he thus labors, he will find after a while that the muscle of the mind, like that of the body, becomes autonomic, a law unto itself; that the intuition with which it works is a safer and surer guide than precepts; and that better and swifter success is reached than the most laborious planning could have gained.

Remember, therefore, always, when you go into the pulpit, that there may be minds before you in the assembly at critical points in their progress, to which your words will give an impulse, in one direction or another, forevermore; that there certainly are minds there adapted to the truth, and sure to take from it an abiding impression. Then your preparation will be thorough and careful. Then you will learn how to handle the themes committed to you with swiftest and with clearest skill; and then whatever you do in the pulpit will be done with earnestness, effectiveness, solemnity.

And FIFTHLY: Remember always to carry with you into the pulpit *a sense of the personal presence of the Master.*

Every minister should do that, whether he reads his sermon from a manuscript, or speaks without notes. But he who preaches without his notes, pre-eminently should do it. The presence of the Master! It is, indeed, a wonderful thing. "Where two or three are gathered together in My name, there am I in the midst of them." That is the promise, the divine declaration; always fulfilled. It sounds like romance. To men of the world it seems no more than a fairy-tale. But it is the essential truth of God's word, the grandest reality of human experience. Here, in this room, this hour, is the Master! in every assembly, where His children meet, and where His kingly word is spoken! By the brook, where the Covenanters worshipped; in the catacombs, where Christian converts first uttered their praises; in the great cathedral, where through all symbols devout spirits discern the Lord; in wood and wilderness, where pilgrim and pioneer sing and pray: everywhere — Christ is present, whom saints adore, and angels serve! And where He is, the place is holy: the service great.

I remember words which I heard thirty years ago, when graduating from the Seminary, which I will read, if you will allow me. They were spoken by one then, and ever since, an honored and eminent pastor in Boston. I have never forgotten them, from that day to this: —

"In a certain congregation there was a hearer of whose presence the preacher was not aware during the delivery of his sermon. When the fact of that hearer's presence was made known to him, it had a great effect upon the preacher. . . . Who was the preacher, and who this hearer?

The preacher I doubt not may have been any young minister present, and the hearer was Jesus Christ. Every time we have preached we have had Him for a hearer. When the great and the learned and the honored of the earth come to hear you, He is there, whose opinion of you, while it is infinitely more important than theirs, will either confirm or reverse their judgment of you. When we meet a few of our flock in that distant school-house on a dark and stormy night, and something whispers, Will you waste your time and strength on these poor people? the Son of God is there to hear what you say to them, and to have an opinion of you for saying it, which is or will hereafter be a greater reward to you than the applauses of a throng. In the bungalow, or under the plantain or the palm, or in those South African huts where you must creep like an animal to get in, remember that you cannot speak in His name but you will speak in His ear." *

* Address of Dr. N Adams: Bib. Sac. vol. ii. p. 709.

Gentlemen: this was not said with reference, especially, to sermons preached without a manuscript. The speaker himself has always, I believe, written his sermons, and has done it with admirable care and skill. But what he says applies with, if possible, a more peremptory force to those who preach without their notes.

Every minister who does this should remember the impressive and powerful truth which these words convey. The thought of the presence of Christ beside him will absolutely expel from his mind all fear of man. He will be undaunted before any criticism, on his manner, or looks, or mode of speaking, if he feels that he is so much in earnest that Christ approves. It will not limit his individuality. It will not disturb the most delicate and sensitive processes of his mind. It will breed in him no unduc self-distrust. Rather, it will invigorate and quicken each power, and make him more natural, and more self-possessed. For God has created every power which we have; has created them for His service;

and the Master recognizes every such power, and bestows upon it His benediction, if it be used in loyalty to Him. He does not disparage it; and we shall not, if we sympathize with Him.

There is no use in trying to make ourselves like others, or to gain for ourselves a special faculty which others have, while we have not. This very variety is in God's plan; and to try to make one man like another, in the pulpit or out of it, is to contravene His design. You might as well try to make a rose resemble in petals a calla-lily; or to make a nightingale, with its plaintive note, whistle military airs like a trained bullfinch. God gives to one a doctrine, to another a song; to one the word of wisdom, to another the word of knowledge; to another prophecy; to another divers kinds of tongues; to another the interpretation of tongues; — and we are simply to hold and use, as sacred to Him, whatever power we possess. He had a use, and a great one, for the rugged, self-willed, impatient Peter, as well as for the sensitive John; for Luke, with his delicate skill in narration, as well as for Paul, with his immense dialectical force. He has offices and services for each of us. What He wants is that we use, to the utmost limit, every power we possess, which He has given, which we have gladly consecrated to Him. A sense of His personal presence with us will, therefore, but make us more wholly natural, self-revealing. It will be like the influence of the sun on the earth, bringing forth the retiring flowers and grasses, and crowning with blossoms all the trees. Whatever of force, whatever of beauty, there is in our minds, will come by means of it into more effective and noble exercise

It will keep us from being secularized in spirit. When not absorbed in the high and vast subjects which the Gospel presents, the mind is apt to grow frigid and unfruitful on its spiritual side. It gets largely interested in other things; literary, social, political movements, scientific discussion, external reform. The richness of experience will then fail in its utterance. The

Christian glow, 'the consecration and the gleam,' will not kindle its speech. But the sense of the personal presence of Christ is a constant corrective to such tendencies. It inspires one to enter the secrets of the Gospel, and to speak from a heart in sympathy with the Lord's. It will make our preaching — to adopt the distinction which some have drawn between John's gospel and those of the Synoptists — pneumatic, not somatic; spiritual, not external. And such a preaching has always a power which the skilfullest arrangement of arguments and of words toils after in vain.

It will inspire in us the true enthusiasm — the 'God within us' — which is like the flame shining within the transparent vase, and revealing itself through all exterior lines and tints. When this is kindled, and constantly burns, in any soul, it makes effort easy, success sure: it is itself a power for God, manifesting His glory through all the faculties which His Spirit illumines.

It will make us glad, this sense of Christ's

presence; it will make us fearless, ardent, devoted. It will unite us in thought with all who have preceded us in the work, preaching His word. We shall see that he is the only true successor of the apostles, who brings the power of Christ, as they did, the Spirit of God, with His promises and truths, to operate on the immortal spirits for which Christ died. We shall feel this office the most august and illustrious on earth; that no other can be ever its equal while time continues; that every thing else, in society and in history, is but the scaffolding to it; that its results will still continue when Waterloo and Trafalgar are wholly forgotten. There will come to us quickening inspiration from the thought, on every side.

Even Paul himself rejoiced to say, when no man stood with him, but all men forsook him: "Notwithstanding, the Lord stood with me, and strengthened me; that by me the preaching might be fully known, and that all the Gentiles might hear." If he needed this sense of Christ's presence, much more do we! If he attained it, so may we. And when we recognize it, with an interior sweetness of certainty, we shall not feel abashed because we have no manuscript before us. To speak for Him will be our impulse. No matter how timid, nervous, self-diffident, we are in ourselves, as we touch His pierced and royal hand we shall be instantly masterful and strong. We can enter, then, that marvellous experience of a derived omnipotence which Paul had, with all his humility, when he wrote to his friends from his prison at Rome: "I can do all things, through Christ which strengtheneth me!"

FINALLY: Gentlemen, *Be perfectly careless of criticism, and expect success.*

You will meet criticism, of course; for you are going out into communities filled with the influence of literary culture and intellectual activity, and in those communities you are to preach. There, indeed, you must learn to preach. You are to learn in the pulpit. You cannot learn to preach in the Seminary, any more than you can learn to swim by stretching yourselves upon this table. You may imitate the motions; but the yielding and buoyant element beneath, is here quite wanting. The lawyer has to learn his skill by practice in the courts; the physician his, not in clinics or laboratories, but in his actual ministry to patients. So you must learn to preach without notes, if you do it at all, in the pulpit, and nowhere else. If these eminent teachers shall have helped you toward it, your memory of them will be sweet and lasting. If any words of mine shall be of the least assistance to you, I shall rejoice to have been permitted to speak them. But you must after all learn for yourselves, and learn by practice.

And in this you will suffer under some disadvantages. You will come into comparison with other, older, perhaps abler men, who have won already facility by practice; who have, very likely, special gifts which you have not, while you may have gifts which are not theirs. You will come into comparison, not with ministers only, but with lawyers, and lecturers — many of them of engaging and eminent parts, who have trained themselves to speak, by incessant endeavor, and with consummate success. You cannot expect to secure the same literary completeness and finish, in a spoken sermon, which you might have gained in one that was written. A spoken sermon is like a rapid and vivid sketch, rather than like a finished picture: vigorous in outline, strong in coloring, with life in its parts, but wanting extreme minuteness of execution in subordinate details. If you want that, and are determined to have it — if you must have every period 'round as Giotto's O,' if you cannot be satisfied without the ivory finish of Carlo Dolci, or the microscopic exactness of Denner's portraits in the Vienna Belvedere, where each wrinkle and hair, one might almost say each pore of the skin, is presented on the canvas — then, assuredly, write your sermons. You cannot gain otherwise what you want. At least I do not believe it possible to give to a free and spoken sermon the same elaborateness and fineness of finish which you may to one written.

But if you are willing to preach correctly, truthfully, energetically, — giving no special thought to the perfection of your finish, except to get as much of it as you can, without being hindered, and to be careless of what you lose, — then speak without writing. Your people will soon come to accept it, and will be stirred by it as they are not by essays. At first they may criticise, and compare your discourses with those of some one who writes with elegance and felicity; but after a while they will choose the utterance through which an eager personal soul is speaking to them its present thought.

I mean that most of them will. Of course, in almost every congregation, there will be some, like Iago, who are "nothing, if not critical." There may be those, I have known such persons, who think themselves wise in exact proportion as they suspect defects in others, and whose chief criterion of their evangelical insight and zeal appears to be the readiness and the rashness of their criticism of sermons. You must expect to encounter such people; and sometimes, no doubt, especially in your earlier years, their criticism will cut you till it hurts.

But remember this: that the criticism is often itself wrong and unreasonable, and then you may laugh at it. So it is everywhere. Hear the criticisms made in a great gallery of pictures, by those who are walking through it: the preference of one for some modern garish French interior, over the tender and harmonious beauty of Correggio's Holy Night; of another for the crude flash and glitter of a recent landscape, over the sweet and sunny splendor of Claude Lorraine. Half the criticism you hear, and nearly all the praise, will be like this; intrinsically worthless. Your ambitious passages may elicit an applause which it were folly to heed; while your best sermons, except by a few, may be quite disregarded.

But then remember, also, that the criticisms upon you will sometimes be just, and such as you may heed with lasting advantage. It will sometimes be said that 'you are too long,' — as you all are just now saying about me; and you will know in yourself that it is so. Then abbreviate, condense; stop, if needful, before you are through. 'You use too many words for your thought;' then compact, and compress. 'Too dry and logical;' then expand, and decorate. 'Too constantly doctrinal;' then preach the evangelical practice, till they want the whole circle of the doctrines of grace to inspire them to attempt it. Get hints and lessons from the sharpest criticism, and strive to correct what it indicates as faults. You will often learn most and best in this way, while it will utterly fail to disturb you; for if your mind is wholly fixed on bringing the water of life to your people, you will not much care, except for their sakes, whether you offer it in a pewter mug or in a silver chalice.

After that, criticism may often help, but it never can hurt you.

Be sure, when it comes, that you take it like a man, and are never overcome by it. Remember what Sheridan said, when he came out from the House of Commons, after they had hissed him: "It's in me, and [with an oath] it shall come out." Omit the oath, but make the vow. If it is in you, and you know it — the conviction of the truth, and the power to express it — determine that it shall at last come out. And let the adverse breath of criticism be to you only what the blast of the storm-wind is to the eagle: a force against him, that lifts him higher.

Remember that ere long the criticism will have wholly passed away, except in the result which it leaves upon your mind, and in the effect which it has upon your preaching. As your people become accustomed to your manner; as they recognize your sincerity, and the earnestness of your work; as they see in your sermons the fruit of study, and feel that you come to them from communion with God; as you get a firm and vital hold on some among them, by meeting their difficulties, cheering their hearts, bracing their wills to a hardier effort, lifting them up to the serener air,—they will no more think of any criticism. You will enter into the liberty you have won. Your pulpit will be to you a home and a throne. You will become your own legislator, as to forms and modes, in subordination only and always to Him for whom you speak to men. And when you come to that experience you will often find that it was the very criticism which stung which brought you to it, and that what has now been utterly forgotten by those who made it, remains with you, in your greater facility, and your continually augmenting power. So be not dismayed by any criticism; but forget it if unjust, and reap from it, if just, whatever of personal benefit you can.

And always, Gentlemen, expect success. I do not mean for yourselves, specially, in the way of fame, personal distinction, lucrative appointments. These may come, or they may not. It is a matter of little consequence. Remember the words of Thackeray, that sad and sombre humorist: "What boots it whether it be Westminster or a little country spire which covers your ashes; or if a few days sooner or later the world forgets you?" * Above all others, the minister should remember the profound and secular wisdom there is in those words of the Master: "For whosoever will save his life shall lose it; but whosoever shall lose his life, for My sake, and the Gospel's, the same shall save it." Influence comes to self-forgetfulness. Honor and power have consecration for their condition. And you will find that the more careless you are of the things which the world esteems success, the more likely you are, if not to reap it, certainly to reach the best results which it could have given, in your experience of happiness and of usefulness.

* Pendennis, vol. i. p. 203.

But expect success in your work for Christ. You have a right to rely upon that; and you need the strength which the foresight of it gives. The suspension-bridge must be anchored at both ends, if one would make it steadfast and strong. Men's souls require to be equally braced. You must not only have an impulse to work, but the sure expectation of success in the work, — your mind and spirit must be poised upon both, — if you would be so tranquil in mind before your people that trains of thought shall pass incessantly on your words, without one painful pause or jar. You have a right to expect such success. The truth of God, which is put into your hands, is the power of God to men's salvation; and never was its power more plainly exhibited than in our own time. The harlots and the dock-thieves along our own wharves, converted to God, now praising Him whom once they cursed, and working for men whom once they wrecked, — there have been no greater triumphs of the Gospel since Christendom began.

And this is the instrument which you have to use, sovereign and swift, the very sword of the Spirit.

Your success may not come at the precise time when you expect it, or in the way which you anticipate. It may not come so that you yourselves shall see it on earth. The Master seemed to men to have realized but small success, in His sublime mission: twelve Apostles, and one of them a traitor; of all the multitudes who had heard His words, His final following very small. Paul, the greatest of human preachers, did not appear to achieve large success: a few scattered and small congregations, in the various Greek cities, with error, impurity, dissension among them, the old Paganism still in part poisoning their life. But out of his labors, and those of his companions, Christendom has come. Out of the work of each faithful minister come consequences of good, immense if unseen. Out of the labor, and sacrifice, and patience, of multitudes of faithful saints and teachers, whose very names we do not know, has come our Christian civilization.

Success is certain, in the end. Then seize it with your hope beforehand. Remember that while you are working Millennium draws nearer; and that it is your privilege to hasten its coming. "Hasting the coming of the day of God;" not hasting *to* it. I trust our Revisers will leave out the "unto:" there is no εἰς before the παρουσίαν. Not suicide, but success, is what the apostle would have us seek.

And even if success does not appear now, or ever on earth, it will surely come in the Beyond. More than once, as I have stood by the grave of a young minister, dead in his prime, — as I have bowed, amazed and baffled, before that event which seems to contradict all economies of God's universe, and to make the cultured power, the garnered knowledge, the vivifying spirit, of no avail, — I have remembered words in the same Address from which I have already quoted, two or three sentences of which you will let me read: —

"We may remember that this life may not be the only term of service in which God may use us to influence others by the communication of our thoughts and feelings. It cannot be that eloquent communication from mind to mind is limited to earth. . . . From your lips, if they have dwelt with peculiar love and power on the doctrines of the cross, may the inhabitants of other worlds learn things yet imperfectly understood by them in the history of Redemption. It may be that you will then be called of God to be employed in wondrous acts of ministry to other worlds, because He can say of you, in remembrance of your earthly attainments and service, 'I know that he can speak well.'" *

Young Gentlemen: in all your life remember this! Let it lift and delight you! Cherish each force, and discipline every noblest power, under its inspiration! Let all work take a lustre from it! And expect the time when the Son of Man, no more invisible, shall be revealed; and when by

* Address of Dr. N. Adams; Bib. Sac. vol. ii. p. 710.

Him shall be opened to you, if here you have been His earnest servants, that grand and bright expanse of Heaven in which may He say to all of us: 'On earth ye have been the rulers over a few things; a few faculties, a few knowledges, a few opportunities: Lo, I will make you rulers over many things, in this kingdom of my Father!' *

Gentlemen: I feel, very keenly, that in what I have said, I have been but giving you a catalogue of my conscious deficiencies. I have not stated a principle, or laid down a precept, that does not now come back to me, as I think of it, with an edge of rebuke. But no matter. These *are* the points where you need to be strong that you may preach, with real success, without writing your sermons. If you are willing to do the work, I think you will be well repaid. You will rescue more time, for larger studies. The fragments and bits of fractured days will become more available. A certain amount of nervous

* Note XXVIII.

waste, in desk and pen-work, will be spared. You will find the mind fruitful, or even luxuriant, at times when it otherwise would lie fallow and sterile. You will reach at times a height of conviction, an intensity of feeling, a supremacy of vision, which you cannot attain except the animation of the assembly be around you. I think you will have a more intimate sense of the presence of the Spirit of God within you, and of the Christ who stands beside you.

But if you undertake the work, remember that you are to give to it time, labor, patience, prayer, invincible resolution; and are not to give it up until you have reached all that success which, within the limitations of nature and of grace, is possible for you. Do it, not in indolence, and not in ambition. Do it, as an offering to the Master, in the spirit of perfect consecration to Him! Do it, as David did his office, when Araunah offered him the threshing-floor, and the wood, and the oxen for his sacrifice, and he said: "I will not offer unto the Lord my God of that which doth cost me nothing." Do it, in the spirit of Paul, when he wrote to the Philippian Christians: "If I be offered — my very life poured out as a libation — upon the sacrifice and service of your faith, I joy, and rejoice with you all."

And so may God accept and bless you in all your ministry, and take you at its end to His own presence!

APPENDIX.

APPENDIX.

A FEW notes have been hastily added to the foregoing lectures, containing, chiefly, brief passages from great writers, which illustrate or emphasize certain points in the text. If leisure had permitted, these might of course have been many times multiplied. Only those are now given which have chanced to be brought to distinct remembrance, in reviewing the general course of thought, or in reading the proof-sheets.

If these richly-woven words of the masters of sentences shall seem to hang on the lectures which precede them like tassels of gold upon a common fabric, it is hoped, nevertheless, that they may in part redeem the poverty which they cannot disguise, but must, undoubtedly, make more apparent.

NOTE I. PAGE 40.

"Every sermon costs me as much time and labor to write as to furnish the matter and subsequent corrections for six or seven. And I have more business to occupy my time and thoughts than you probably suppose. When you see me lounging about the garden, and pruning a rose-bush, you probably suppose that I am thinking of nothing else; when, perhaps, I am deliberating on some weighty matter, on which I have to decide." — *Letter of Abp. Whately: Life*, vol. ii. p. 226.

NOTE II. PAGE 46.

Macaulay has pictured two different masters of the English language, in passages of his Essays which may be usefully read together: —

"His [Dryden's] command of language was immense. With him died the secret of the old poetical diction of England, — the art of producing rich effects by familiar words. . . . On the other hand, he was the first writer under whose skilful management the scientific vocabulary fell into natural and pleasing verse. In this department he succeeded as completely as his contemporary Gibbons succeeded in the similar enterprise of carving the most delicate flowers from heart of oak. The toughest and most knotty parts of language became ductile at his touch." — *Essay, on Dryden.*

"The style of Bunyan is delightful to every reader, and invaluable as a study to every person who wishes to obtain a wide command over the English language. The vocabulary is the vocabulary of the common people. There is not an expression, if we except a few technical terms of theology, which would puzzle the rudest peasant. . . Yet no writer has said more exactly what he meant to say. For magnificence, for pathos, for vehement exhortation, for subtle disquisition, for every purpose of the poet, the orator, and the divine, this homely dialect, the dialect of plain working men, was perfectly sufficient." — *Essay, on Pilgrim's Progress.*

NOTE III. PAGE 47.

From the multitude of illustrations in Shakspeare of his keen sense of the strength or the music of words, two may be taken, the contrast between them emphasizing each: —

"I stood like a man at a mark, with a whole army shooting at me: she speaks poniards, and every word stabs." — *Much Ado about Nothing*, act ii. sc. 1.

"His eye begets occasion for his wit:
For every object that the one doth catch,
The other turns to a mirth-moving jest;
Which his fair tongue, conceit's expositor,
Delivers in such apt and gracious words,
That aged ears play truant at his tales,
And younger hearings are quite ravished,
So sweet and voluble is his discourse."

Love's Labor's Lost, act ii. sc. 1

Note IV. Page 47.

"It was the Arcadia [of Sidney] which first taught to the contemporary writers that inimitable interweaving and contexture of words, that bold and unshackled use and application of them, — that art of giving to language, appropriated to objects the most common and trivial, a kind of acquired and adventitious loftiness, and to diction in itself noble and elevated a sort of super-added dignity, — that power of ennobling the sentiments by the language and the language by the sentiments, — which so often excites our admiration in perusing the writers of the age of Elizabeth." — *Retrospective Review; quoted by Hallam: Lit. Hist. of Europe*, part 2, chap. vii.

NOTE V. PAGE 49.

"The collocation of words is so artificial in Shakspeare and Milton, that you may as well think of pushing a brick out of a wall with your fore-finger, as attempt to remove a word out of any of their finished passages." — *Coleridge's Table Talk*, July 3, 1833.

Perhaps as fair an account as can be given of some of Coleridge's own sentences is contained in this later remark of his about Shakspeare: —

"Shakspeare's intellectual action is wholly unlike that of Ben Jonson, or Beaumont and Fletcher. The latter see the totality of a sentence or passage, and then project it entire. Shakspeare goes on creating, and evolving B. out of A., and C. out of B., and so on, just as a serpent moves, which makes a fulcrum of its own body, and seems forever twisting and untwisting its own strength." — *Table Talk*, March 5, 1834.

NOTE VI. PAGE 52.

"Stylus optimus et præstantissimus dicendi effector ac magister; neque injuria. Nam si subitam et fortuitam orationem commentatio et cogitatio facile vincit; hanc ipsam profecto assidua ac diligens scriptura superabit. Omnes enim, sive artis sunt loci, sive ingenii cujusdam atque prudentiæ, qui modo insunt in ea re, de qua scribimus, anquirentibus nobis, omnique acie ingenii contemplantibus ostendunt se et occurrunt; omnesque sententiæ, verbaque omnia, quæ sunt cujusque generis maxime illustria, sub acumen styli subeant et succedant necesse est; tum ipsa collocatio conformatioque verborum perficitur in scribendo, non poetico, sed quodam oratorio numero et modo." — CICERO: *De Oratore*, lib. I, cap. xxxiii.

How vividly the effect of careful and habitual writing upon unwritten speech, in imparting to it the law of its own movement, is illustrated in the well-known figure which closes the same chapter: —

"Ut concitato navigio, quum remiges inhibuerunt, retinet tamen ipsa navis motum et cursum suum, intermisso impetu pulsuque remorum: sic in oratione perpetua, quum scripta deficiunt, parem tamen obtinet oratio reliqua cursum, scriptorum simiItiudine et vi concitata."

NOTE VII. PAGE 63.

"It's a great mistake to think any thing too profound or rich for a popular audience. No train of thought is too deep, or subtle, or grand — but the manner of presenting it to their untutored minds should be peculiar. It should be presented in anecdote, or sparkling truism, or telling illustration, or stinging epithet; always in some concrete form, never in a logical, abstract, syllogistic shape." — CHOATE: *Parker's Reminiscences*, p. 261.

NOTE VIII. PAGE 66.

"Be a man's vocation what it may, his rule should be to do its duties perfectly, to do the best he can, and thus to make perpetual progress in his art. In other words, Perfection should be proposed. . . .

"Difficulty is the element, and resistance the true work, of a man." — CHANNING: vol. ii. p. 385.

Note IX. Page 76.

"Our ideas are so infinitely enlarged by Revelation, the eye of reason has so wide a prospect into Eternity, the notions of a Deity are so worthy and refined, and the accounts we have of a state of happiness or misery so clear and evident, that the contemplation of such objects will give our discourse a noble vigor, an invincible force, beyond the power of any human consideration." — *The Spectator*, No. 633.

Note X. Page 80.

"When the sermon is good we need not much concern ourselves about the form of the pulpit. But sermons cannot always be good; and I believe that the temper in which the congregation set themselves to listen may be in some degree modified by their perception of fitness or unfitness, impressiveness or vulgarity, in the disposition of the place appointed for the speaker, — not to the same degree, but somewhat in the same way, that they may be influenced by his own gestures or expression, irrespective of the sense of what he says. . . . But if once we begin to regard the preacher, whatever his faults, as a man sent with a message to us, which it is a matter of life or death whether we hear or refuse, . . . we shall look with changed eyes upon that frippery of gay furniture about the place from which the message of judgment must be delivered, which either breathes upon the dry bones that they may live, or, if ineffectual, remains recorded in condemnation, perhaps against the utterer and listener alike, but assuredly against one of them. We shall not so easily bear with the silk and gold upon the seat of judgment, nor with ornament of oratory in the mouth of the messenger: we shall wish that his words may be simple, even when they are sweetest, and the place from which he speaks like a marble rock in the desert, about which the people have gathered in their thirst." — RUSKIN: *Stones of Venice*, vol. ii., chap. ii., §§ 13, 14.

"The successive pulpits of the Abbey, if not equally expressive of the changes which it has witnessed, carry on the sound of many voices, heard with delight and wonder in their time. No vestige remains of the old mediæval platform whence the Abbots urged the reluctant Court of Henry III. to the Crusades. But we have still the fragile structure from which Cranmer must have preached at the coronation and funeral of his royal godson; and the more elaborate carving of that which resounded with the passionate appeals, at one time of

Baxter, Howe, and Owen, at other times of Heylin, Williams, South, and Barrow. . . . The marble pulpit in the nave, given in 1859 to commemorate the beginning of the Special Services through which Westminster led the way in re-animating the silent naves of our cathedrals, has thus been been the chief vehicle of the varied teaching of those who have been well called 'the People's preachers:' 'vox quidem dissona, sed una religio.' — STANLEY: *Memorials of West. Abbey*, ch. vi. p. 551.

NOTE XI. PAGE 93.

"The sun, which we want, ripens wits, as well as fruits." — MILTON: *Hist. of Britain*, book iii.

"To be free-minded, and cheerfully disposed, at hours of meat and of sleep and of exercise, is one of the best precepts of long lasting." — *Bacon's Essays*, xxx.

"Happily for my eyes, I have always closed my studies with the day, and commonly with the morning; and a long, but temperate, labor has been accomplished, without fatiguing either the mind or body." — GIBBON'S *Memoirs*, p. 117.

Note XII. Page 96.

"The most wearisome details of questions, now this long while settled and forgotten, receive a suffusion of interest and color from the constant play around them of wide and rich human wisdom. Whatever he handled . . . all was treated with that nobility of idea and expression which mere talent is invariably the better for studying, but which is only inborn, familiar, and perfect, in a few men of fine genius and deep morality of nature. Passion left flaws to offend a fastidious taste, and too frequently marked his gravity with exaggeration, and his humor with clumsiness. But these were mainly accidents of atmosphere. Notwithstanding them, we look in vain elsewhere in the history of English politics for the illumination of such questions as those before us, by such amplitude of knowledge, united to so much comprehension, force, and elevation." — Morley: *Study of Edmund Burke*, p. 167.

"His wonderful ability for comprehending and reasoning, his quickness of apprehension, his faculty for analyzing a subject to its elements, for seizing on the essential points, for going back to principles and forward to consequences, and for bringing out into an intelligible and sometimes very obvious form what appeared obscure or perplexed, remained unaltered to the last. This noble intellect, thus seen with a diminished lustre of imagination, suggested the idea of a lofty eminence, raising its form and summit clear and bare towards the sky, losing nothing of its imposing aspect by absence of the wreaths of tinctured clouds, which may have invested it at another season. . . . He was eminently successful on subjects of an elevated order, which he would expand and illustrate in a manner which sustained them to the high level of their dignity. This carried him near some point of the border of that awful darkness which encompasses, on all sides, our little glimmering field of knowledge; and then it might be seen how aware he was of his approach, how cautiously, or shall I say instinctively, he was held aloof, how sure not to abandon the ground of evidence, by a hazardous incursion of conjecture or imagination into the unknown. He would indicate how near, and in what direction, lay the shaded frontier; but dared not, did not seem even tempted, to invade its 'majesty of darkness.'" — JOHN FOSTER: *Observations on Robert Hall.*

Note XIII. Page 100.

"You have letters, but no learning, that understand so many languages, turn over so many volumes, and yet are but asleep when all is done." — Milton, *to Salmasius.*

Note XIV. Page 103.

"I call, therefore, a complete and generous education that which fits a man to perform, justly, liberally, and magnanimously, all the offices, both private and public, of peace and war." — Milton, *on Education.*

Note XV. Page 106.

"Great scholar he was none, the Latin Testament, gotten by heart, being the master-piece of his learning; nor any studied lawyer, never long living, if admitted, in the Inns of Court; nor experienced soldier, though necessity cast him on that calling when the Duke of Bourbon besieged Rome; nor courtier in his youth, till bred in the Court, as I may call it, of Cardinal Wolsey: and yet, that of the lawyer in him so helped the scholar, that of the soldier the lawyer, that of the courtier the soldier, and that of the traveller so perfected all the rest, — being no stranger to Germany, well acquainted with France, most familiar with Italy — that the result of all together made him for endowments eminent, not to say admirable." — THOMAS FULLER: *on Cromwell, Earl of Essex. Church Hist. of Britain*, cent. 16, book v.

NOTE XVI. PAGE 108.

"Of eloquence it has been eloquently said: 'Eloquentia sicut flamma, materie alitur, motu excitatur, urendo clarescit.' Mr. Pitt thus happily rendered the passage: 'It is of eloquence as of a flame: it requires matter to feed it, motion to excite it, and it brightens as it burns.'" — *Preface to Lord Russell's Life of Charles James Fox.*

NOTE XVII. PAGE 118.

Yet there are admirable sermons to which we may almost apply Goethe's words about the characters of Shakspeare, as quoted by Carlyle: —

"His characters are like watches with dial-plates of transparent crystal: they show you the hour, like others, and the inward mechanism also is all visible." — *On Heroes, Lect.* 3.

Note XVIII. Page 121.

It is hazardous to introduce extended descriptions of natural scenery into sermons, lest the personal experience with which they are connected be rather hidden than illustrated by them; and lest — as has sometimes happened — the sermon itself shall seem to have been constructed with reference to them, as if a house had been planned to match a mantel-piece. But, occasionally, they add to a discourse a vivid and memorable moral force, as well as rare pictorial beauty.

The following passages from a modern sermon illustrate, perhaps, both the danger and the gain: —

"The more you lose your isolated self, and the thoughts and feelings which cluster round it, and take instead into you the thoughts and feelings of others, the richer and the more varied, the more complex and the more interesting, and therefore the more vividly individual, becomes your being. . . .

"It was my fortune last year, in going from Torcello to Venice, to be overtaken by one of the whirlwinds which sometimes visit the south. It was a dead calm, but the whole sky, high overhead, was covered with a pall of purple, sombre and smooth, but full of scarlet threads. Across this, from side to side, as if darted by two invisible armies, flew at every instant flashes of forked lightning; but so lofty was the storm — and this gave a hushed terror to the scene — that no thunder was heard. Beneath this sky the lagoon water was dead purple, and the weedy shoals left naked by the tide dead scarlet. The only motion in the sky was far away to the south, where a palm-tree of pale mist seemed to rise from the water, and to join itself above to a self-infolding mass of seething cloud. We reached a small island and landed. An instant after, as I stood on the parapet of the fortification, amid the breathless silence, this pillar of cloud, ghostly white, and relieved against the violet darkness of the sky, its edge as clear as if cut with a knife, came rushing forward over the lagoon, driven by the spirit of wind, which, hidden within it, whirled and coiled its column into an endless spiral.

The wind was only there, at its very edge there was not a ripple; but as it drew near our island it seemed to be pressed down upon the sea, and, unable to resist the pressure, opened out like a fan in a foam of vapor. Then with a shriek which made every nerve thrill with excitement, the imprisoned wind leapt forth, the water of the lagoon, beaten flat, was torn away to the depth of half an inch, and as the cloud of spray and wind smote the island, it trembled all over like a ship struck by a great wave. We seemed to be in the very heart of the universe at a moment when the thought of the universe was most sublime. . . . It is in such a moment when, as it were, you find your individuality outside of you, in the being of the universe, that you are most individual, and most able to *feel* your being, though not to ***think*** it." — STOPFORD A. BROOKE: *Sermon on Individuality.*

NOTE XIX. PAGE 148.

"Truth is the beginning of every good to the gods, and of every good to man: and he who would be blessed and happy should be from the first a partaker of the truth, that he may live a true man as long as possible, for then he can be trusted; but he is not to be trusted who loves voluntary falsehood, and he who loves involuntary falsehood, is a fool." — PLATO: *Laws*, book v, sec. 730.

Compare with this the loftier saying of a Christian philosopher: —

"The energies of the intellect, increase of insight, and enlarging views, are necessary to keep alive the substantial faith in the heart. They are the appointed fuel to the sacred fire. In the state of perfection all other faculties may, perhaps, be swallowed up in love; but it is on the wings of the cherubim, which the ancient Hebrew doctors interpreted as meaning the powers and efforts of the intellect, that we must first be borne up to the 'pure Empyrean;' and it must be seraphs, and not the hearts of poor mortals, that can burn unfueled and self-fed." — COLERIDGE: *Lay Sermons*, p. 156, Burlington Ed.

NOTE XX. PAGE 152.

"This singular treatise contains a profusion of epithets, new-created words, paraphrases, and repetitions, conveyed in long and intricate periods. He clouds his meaning by his gorgeous rhetoric: never content with illustrating his sentiment by an adapted simile, he is perpetually abandoning his subject to pursue his imagery. He illustrates his illustrations, till he has forgotten both their meaning and applicability. Hence his style is an endless tissue of figures, which he never leaves till he has converted every metaphor into a simile, and every simile into a wearisome episode. . . . The whole is a confused medley of great and exuberant genius, wasting and burlesquing uncommon powers." — TURNER'S *Hist. Anglo Saxons*, vol. iii., pp. 351, 352. (On Aldhelm, Abbot of Malmsbury.)

NOTE XXI. PAGE 154.

This reference to Dr. Emmons, made upon the imperfect recollection of the moment, does not represent with entire correctness his remark; and as he was a very exact man it is better to give his apothegm with exactness: —

"Style is only the frame to hold our thoughts. It is like the sash of a window; a heavy sash will obscure the light. The object is to have as little sash as will hold the lights, that we may not think of the frame, but have the most light." — *Prof. Park's Memoir*, p. 328.

The Doctor himself did not approve of preaching without notes; and if he had foreseen that he was ever to be referred to in a lecture upon the subject it would very likely have added fresh emphasis — if that were possible — to his mild declaration that "the most important requisites for an extemporaneous preacher are ignorance, impudence, and presumption." Yet his biographer says of one celebrated passage in a sermon of his: "There are internal signs that his lightning-like comments may have been made *extempore* in that paragraph. The electric spirit of them has vanished from the words as they appear in type." (p. 330).

Even with him, then, it was the unwritten word, not the written, which flamed and burned.

NOTE XXII. PAGE 156.

The whole familiar and noble passage may well be quoted: —

"For me, readers, although I cannot say that I am utterly untrain'd in those rules which best rhetoricians have given, or unacquainted with those examples which the prime authors of eloquence have written, in any learned tongue; yet true Eloquence I find to be none but the serious and hearty love of truth: and that whose mind soever is fully possest with a fervent desire to know good things, and with the dearest charity to infuse the knowledge of them into others, when such a man would speak, his words (by what I can express) like so many nimble and airy servitors trip about him at command, and in well-order'd files, as he would wish, fall aptly into their own places." —*Apology for Smectymnuus.*

Note XXIII. Page 158.

"The greatest thoughts are wronged, if not linked with beauty; and they win their way most surely and deeply into the soul when arrayed in this their natural and fit attire. . . . Thus outward beauty is akin to something deeper and unseen, is the reflection of spiritual attributes." — Channing: *Works*, vol. ii. p. 366.

Note XXIV. Page 172.

"Our great thoughts, our great affections, the truths of our life, never leave us. Surely, they cannot separate from our consciousness; shall follow it whithersoever that shall go, and are of their nature Divine and immortal." — THACKERAY, *Esmond*, book iii. chap. vi.

NOTE XXV. PAGE 174.

"Sooty Manchester, — it too is built on the infinite abysses; over-spanned by the skyey firmaments; and there is birth in it, and death in it; — and it is every whit as wonderful, as fearful, unimaginable, as the oldest Salem or prophetic city. Go or stand, in what time, in what place we will, are there not Immensities, Eternities, over us, around us, in us:

'Solemn before us,
Veiled, the dark Portal,
Goal of all mortal: —
Stars silent rest o'er us,
Graves under us silent.'"

CARLYLE: *Past and Present*, book iii. chap. xv.

NOTE XXVI. PAGE 176.

"In all the accounts one reads of myrrh, frankincense, and other 'medicinal gums,' one always finds different qualities mentioned; the *best* being what exudes spontaneously, and not by tapping or boiling down. And so it is with apothegms. If a man taps himself to draw them out, he will be the more likely to sacrifice truth to antithesis." — *Letter of Abp. Whately: Life*, vol. ii. p. 312.

NOTE XXVII. PAGE 178.

Milton's good word for occasional sarcasm is certainly just: —

"Even this vein of laughing, as I could produce out of grave authors, hath ofttimes a strong and sinewy force in teaching and confuting." — MILTON: *on Remonstrant's Defence.*

But the maxim of Lord Bacon seems always the best one for the pulpit: —

"As for jest, there be certain things which ought to be privileged from it; namely, religion, matters of state, great persons, any man's present business of importance, and any case that deserveth pity. Yet there be some that think their wits have been asleep, except they dart out something that is piquant, and to the quick. That is a vein which should be bridled:

"Parce, puer, stimulis, et fortius utere loris." — BACON'S *Essays*, xxxii.

NOTE XXVIII. PAGE 203.

"The rugged gentleness, the wit whose glory
 Flash'd like a sword, because its edge was keen,
The fine antithesis, the flowing story; —
 Beneath such things the sainthood is not seen,

"Till in the hours when the wan hand is lifted
 To take the bread and wine, through all the mist
Of mortal weariness our eyes are gifted
 To see a quiet radiance caught from Christ;

"Till from the pillow of the thinker, lying
 In weakness, comes the teaching, then best taught,
That the true crown for any soul in dying
 Is Christ, not genius, and is faith, not thought.

"O Death, for all thy darkness, grand unveiler
Of lights on lights above Life's shadowy place,
Just as the night, that makes our small world paler,
Shows us the star-sown amplitudes of space!

"O strange discovery! Land that knows no bounding,
Isles far off hail'd, bright seas without a breath,
What time the white sail of the soul is rounding
The misty cape — the promontory Death!"

REV. WILLIAM ALEXANDER:
On the Death of Archbishop Whately

www.ingramcontent.com/pod-product-compliance
Lightning Source LLC
LaVergne TN
LVHW050526100826
845148LV00002B/459